Scrooge and Marley

Karl F. Hollenbach

Published by internet marketing KY, LLC
d/b/a Books, Authors, And Artists
Louisville, KY, U.S.A.

Electronic publishing by internet marketing KY, LLC,
November 2012

CreateSpace ISBN: 0615728502
CreateSpace ISBN-13: 978-0615728506

"I'm as light as a feather,
as happy as an angel,
as merry as a schoolboy,
as giddy as a drunken old man!"

EBENEZER SCROOGE
A CHRISTMAS CAROL

". . his glimpse of the Invisible World . . ."

CONTENTS

PREFACE

My first opportunity to hear about *A CHRISTMAS CAROL* occurred in the sixth grade, seven decades ago, when Eva Wright gave a book report "about ghosts." Fascinated by Dickens' wonderful story of redemption—although at that time I didn't know what that was all about—I asked my parents to buy the two-disc record set with Basil Rathbone portraying Scrooge. Enchanted, I listened to Marley's ghost and two of the spirits speak through my wind-up victrola.

More than four decades later, I had the opportunity as a teacher at Saint Brigid Elementary School in Vine Grove, Kentucky to introduce *A CHRISTMAS CAROL* to junior high students during the three weeks between Thanksgiving and Christmas.

During the seven years I taught at Saint Brigid, the students read *A CHRISTMAS CAROL* aloud each of those three "full-of-wonder" weeks. Opinions about Marley being a real ghost and interpretations of Scrooge's being visited by three spirits allowed for Socratic Learning ("What do you think. . . ?" and "Why do you suppose. . . ?")

With the hope for Charles Dickens' approval, I submit, dear reader, for your reading pleasure, *SCROOGE AND MARLEY*.

Karl F. Hollenbach

MARLEY'S GHOST

Marley's ghost, from Charles Dickens: *A Christmas Carol. In Prose. Being a Ghost Story of Christmas*. With Illustrations by John Leech. London: Chapman & Hall, 1843. First edition.
Attribution:
John Leech [Public domain], via Wikimedia Commons
http://commons.wikimedia.org/wiki/File:Marley%27s_Ghost-John_Leech,_1843.jpg

PROLOGUE

Ebenezer Scrooge considered Christmas a "humbug." Uncharitable to solicitors for funds for the poor, his only concern was whether the poorhouse was no longer open. He grudgingly gave his clerk Christmas day off. When his nephew wished him a "Merry Christmas," he responded, "And good day to you, sir." In short, Scrooge was not a pleasant person.

On Christmas Eve Scrooge was visited by the ghost of his dead, miserly, and selfish partner, Jacob Marley, who had to trudge through the spirit world encumbered by chains. Marley told Scrooge that three spirits would visit him, and if he was to be saved from an even worse fate than was Marley's, he had to meet these three spirits.

At twelve midnight a childlike figure appeared, saying she was the Spirit of Christmas Past and showed Scrooge scenes from his past. The second spirit, the Spirit of Christmas Present, a huge, jovial man, dressed in red and green, took Scrooge to the homes of those people that should have been dear to him.

These scenes touched Scrooge. And he shed tears. Visited by the third spirit, Scrooge said he feared it most. The Spirit of Christmas Future showed Scrooge his own lonely death, with no one grieving at his grave.

A changed man, Scrooge yelled, "I don't know what to do! I am as happy as an angel, I am as merry as a schoolboy, I am as giddy as a drunken man. A Merry Christmas to everybody!" The Spirit of Christmas had made Scrooge a different man from the one he had been.

I

Scrooge had become another man from what he was.

That must be understood in the beginning; otherwise, what follows would be idle fancy, a whimsical figment of the imagination, a fiction of the mind.

Scrooge was another man from what he was. Now children clustered about him as if he were an incarnation of St. Nicholas. When, from the deep pockets of his coat, he produced a piece of rock candy for each youngster; and adults confided in him as if he were their confessor, accepting his good counsel, and more than occasionally, when the person was hard pressed, thanking him for the pound note he pressed into their palm.

When he met young Brigid Hawkins on the street, he nodded his head slightly, tipped his top hat with his right index finger, and smiled more with his eyes than his lips. The child she carried in her arms that first time Scrooge spoke to her – while she shopped for her family's twelfth-night celebration – now clutched her hand and smiled in anticipation of the candy that Scrooge took from a small bag in his coat pocket.

"How good it is to see you again, Mrs. Hawkins."

She smiled and touched the cuff of his coat sleeve. "Thank you so much, Mr. Scrooge, for getting Albert his new job."

Scrooge held the candy in front of him with a questioning look in his eyes. Mrs. Hawkins smiled and nodded her head yes.

Primarily young adults sought out Scrooge, such as George Frobisher, the son of one of the Scrooge's renters. He had married Polly Cotters after asking Scrooge for his opinion, as to whether it would be better to establish himself firmly in business, and own a home before proposing to her. "Marry her!" Marry her, my boy!" A guest at their wedding, Scrooge gave them two silver napkin rings engraved with "Polly" and "George," with a tiny heart between the names.

Scrooge was a different man. Even his physical appearance was different. He still stooped when he walked, but now, there was a slight lilt. A kind of rhythmical cadence that sometimes seemed like prancing, and at other times – had he been a younger man – as swaggering. Children laughed ¬with him, not at him, when he jaunted past them. While their parents smiled at this doddering old gentlemen who's "Good Morning, my dear," and "Good Day, Sir!" and "Lovely day, isn't it?" persuaded them that he was in his own world and was oblivious to all the problems of theirs. In one sense, they were right. He was in a world of his own. Not unlike the young suitor, whose sweetheart has accepted his offer of marriage, except Scrooge was not in love with someone, but everyone. He awoke each morning with the expectation of adventure, and whether the sun shone or the rain poured, he raised his bedroom window and flung open the shutters, before spreading his arms and inhaling the cool morning air. Although he lived over a mile from the church, the cross on its steeple became the focus for his silent prayer of thanks each morning, even when it snowed.

They were right also in the sense that the world of Spirit, in which Scrooge now communed each moment, had very few other communicants in busy London, so it would be correct to say that it was his own world. This difference in Scrooge, his being another man from what he had been, occurred last Christmas Eve. When all the flaws, misdeeds, strayings, and errors of all his actions converged on his soul, like the rays of the sun through a lens. And his long journey to darkness reversed in a burst of joy to light.

The quarters he lived in had changed little, but certain warmth radiated through the once damp, dingy rooms. The drapes were now pulled to the side each morning and sunlight crept into hidden spaces that had been black for ages. In winter, a fire blazed in the sitting room as well as in Scrooge's sleeping quarters. The warmth permeating his quarters was not all from nature, but also from a glowing heart that relished each living breath, each day, each hour.

It was in his routine that the other man Scrooge had become was readily observed. Now he walked two blocks farther to his office each day in order to buy a flower for his lapel from the girl on the corner. And he intentionally came to his office everyday fifteen minutes after Bob Cratchet had opened it.

He no longer ate by himself in the "Cat and Fiddle" pub, but was now part of the "old gang" of aged gentlemen, who either as widowers or bachelors, gathered each day to talk more than they ate and laugh, almost as much as they drank. Alfred always greeted Scrooge and showed him to the booth he "kept for Mr. Scrooge." He would take Scrooge's hat and coat, hang them up for him, and always suggest the special of the day, which Scrooge usually ordered, not wishing to discourage Alfred's enthusiasm in his eloquent descriptions of "mouth-watering, cut-with-your-fork beef pie, fresh country made bubbles and squeak, and most blessed Holy Cross plum pudding." Alfred appreciated the coins Scrooge always left on the table, but he gave him special attention, because Scrooge was a different man from the one who before had eaten alone, had said little, and had left only crumbs on the table.

Scrooge was a different man, not because he feared hell, but because he had found the joy of heaven. The church bell struck twelve noon. "We're closing up early, Bob Cratchet." Not completely adjusted to Scrooge's recent whimsical behavior regarding business, Cratchet thought it best to mention the early hour of the day. "It's only noon, Mr. Scrooge."

"And time for you to be leaving for home, Bob. I'm sure Mrs. Cratchet will have many chores for you." Cratchet smiled and nodded his head. "I'm looking forward to Christmas Eve dinner with you and your family, Bob. It is most kind of you to have invited me. Now, begone!"

The door was not closed but a moment, before two gentlemen entered, the same two who had solicited funds for the poor the previous Christmas Eve from Scrooge and had been rudely dismissed by him. "Ah, Mr. Chelmsford is it not?" said Scrooge. "And"—he hesitated—"Mr. Prynne. Come in gentlemen. I have my pledge here on my desk, ready to give it to you with much joy in my heart. I thank you for taking your time during the holidays to help raise funds for the needy."

After leaving Scrooge's office, Prynne said, "Quite a difference from our visit last year." "Indeed," said Chelmsford. "The chambers are still rather moldy and dusty, but such a change in a man seemed impossible. Look at his pledge." They both smiled, their faith in miracles upheld.

Scrooge looked at the clock. They promised to be at his office at 1 o'clock. No earlier. That was one of the reasons Scrooge had told Bob Cratchet to be on his way home at noon. The sign was complete, and it would only take a short time to hang it in place of the old sign, they had told him. The old sign, "Scrooge and Marley" needed to be repainted long ago, but now in its place would hang a new sign, "Scrooge, Marley, and Cratchet." Scrooge intended to inform Cratchet and his family this evening, when Scrooge would be their guest for dinner, that Bob was now a partner. The sign was an extra surprise for Cratchet when he came to the office after Christmas.

It was 3 o'clock when Scrooge locked the door. He stepped back and admired the new sign. Marley would approve. That is, the Marley of last Christmas Eve. The "old" Marley – if one is permitted to call the youth of an individual "old" – had kept far tighter purse strings than had penny-pinching "old" Scrooge. He was not sure Marley would consider the fancy, golden border around the four sides of the sign necessary, but Scrooge had requested it.

The green grocer had wrapped three baskets of assorted fruits in Christmas decorations that morning at Scrooge's request. Scrooge was so pleased with them, that he gave Mr. Owen three extra shillings later that afternoon, and offered Mr. Owen's young son three shillings to deliver one basket to the home of Miss Nettie Straw, who was Scrooge's charwoman; one basket to Mrs. Dilbert, his laundress, and one basket to Miss Charlotte Cope, who brought him breakfast each morning and at night, left warm gruel spiced with raisins by the fireplace. All three of the baskets had a card with "Merry Christmas Ebenezer Scrooge" written by his own hand. He was as pleased with himself as all three of them were surprised by the gift, and shocked by the giver.

Scrooge arrived at the "Cat and Fiddle" Pub the same time as he normally did. However, this time, when Alfred offered to take Scrooge's coat and hat, Scrooge raised his hand. "I'm eating Christmas Eve dinner at a friend's home, Albert. I want you to have this. Merry Christmas, Albert." Like the three women, Albert was surprised that Scrooge would not be eating at the pub tonight, and shocked at the five-pound note pressed in his palm. Before he could say a word, Scrooge had turned about and departed.

The owner of the toy store had never met Mr. Scrooge before, and was surprised at this kindly old gentleman taking such pleasure in buying a small drum and flute, a fancy dressed doll, a small music box, and a chess set with Napoleon and the French as one set of pieces, and the Duke of Wellington and the English, the other set. Bob Cratchet had mentioned once that he and his son Peter played chess often.

Bob Cratchet's two daughters, Martha and Belinda, were too old for toys. Scrooge knew that Martha was apprenticed to a milliner. He had asked his niece, Kathleen, if she would go to the millinery shop to purchase two bonnets. She was to ask for Martha and say she wanted two bonnets for two girls about Martha's age. Which bonnets would Martha select?

Kathleen had bought the two bonnets that Martha selected and placed them in special boxes, wrapped in green paper and tied with a large red ribbon. There was just enough time for Scrooge to go to his nephew and niece's house for the two boxes. Offering the toy-store owner's son, Neil, two shillings to carry the packages of toys. He arrived at 5 o'clock, leaving him half an hour before he was expected at Bob Cratchet's home. An extra shilling lightened Neil's task of carrying two more boxes.

Peter Cratchet helped Neil place the colorful Christmas boxes in the corner of the house by the table, upon which a crèche with faded colors still sparkled in the light of many candles. Bob Cratchet shook Scrooge's hand for such a long time, saying how pleased the family was to have him as a guest for dinner, that Scrooge finally had to say, "May I come in?"

The meal had been a success, much to Mrs. Cratchet's pleasure, and the gifts Scrooge brought proved "just what each of the six children wanted." Tim was walking now without a crutch, because of the doctor Scrooge had engaged, but he was still very thin, and that concerned Scrooge. He was pleased to hear Bob Cratchet inform him that Scrooge's nephew Fred, who was a barrister, had arranged a position for Peter in his own office.

The church bells rang 7 o'clock and Scrooge took his leave. Bob helped him with his overcoat. "Will you be going to church tomorrow morning, Bob?"

"Why yes, Mr. Scrooge. The entire family."

"May I accompany you tomorrow morning?"

"Why yes! We would be delighted. Martha, Mr. Scrooge will be going to church with us tomorrow morning!"

Scrooge smiled and patted Bob on the arm. "Good night, Bob. Merry Christmas. A very merry Christmas."

A short distance from the Cratchet home, Scrooge again walked the same narrow lane that led to his chambers, as he did that lonely night a year ago this very eve. Then, as now, the snow slapped against his cheeks, but now the warm glow within his heart made him oblivious to its sting. He was about to reenact the wonder of that evening, when a bitter old man found joy within his heart.

He ungloved his hand to easily retrieve the cold key in the deep pocket of his coat. He blew his warm breath on the key and his hand. There in front of him was the door – more correctly, the doorknocker – which heralded the beginning of his turnabout, his transformation, when the face of his dead partner, Jacob Marley, materialized in the center of the doorknocker exactly a year ago tonight.

He squinted his eyes, moved within a few inches of the brass doorknocker, and then sighed. Just a knocker. Nothing more. He took the bit of holly that Belinda had placed in the buttonhole of his coat, and stuck in under the knocker. Anxious to relive those special hours of last year, Scrooge fumbled with the key, pushed back the creaky door, and reached for the candle on the table, by the side of the door.

Scrooge's chambers were on the second floor of the large building, that he had inherited from the estate of Jacob Marley. Marley had made Scrooge his sole executor and beneficiary. Scrooge had moved from his smaller rented quarters into these present larger chambers, which had been Marley's. The other rooms were rented out and the basement became a warehouse for wines. Marley's death had enhanced Scrooge's not-so-small estate three-fold; he was sole

owner of "Scrooge and Marley", sole owner of his large
sole beneficiary of all the properties Marley had accu
three decades.

Scrooge had told Charlotte Cope that morning, when she brought
him his breakfast, that he would be late coming home that evening, --
he would be "dining with friends", he proudly proclaimed – and she
need not leave his usual gruel and raisins by the fireplace, nor need
she light the fire. He expected, therefore, that his chambers would be
cold and dark, as he unlocked the door.

The room was bright and warm! Had Charlotte forgotten? He
removed his hat and muffler and gazed at the bright fire burning in
the fireplace, going over his conversation with her. Surely, she
understood. He had been quite clear; she did not have to bring him
his gruel that evening or make a fire. Even more puzzling was the
fact that no bowl of gruel sat by the fireplace or on the table. He
walked towards the fire, and then, he saw. There in his own chair
facing the fireplace, sat Marley!

II

What Scrooge called Marley, you, dear reader, after a moment of shock—certainly, surprise—would describe as a pale blue haze that dripped down the floor in two streams, through which the buttons on the back of the chair could be seen. With the imagination of a child, that sees lions and tigers and myriad faces in the ever-changing clouds, one might, by squinting one's eyes, see the outline of a coat, trousers, and possibly slippers, as well as the features of a human face.

Last Christmas Eve, Scrooge had encountered the ghosts of his dead partner, with all the cumbersome accessories of past misdeeds and missed chances, attached to a great chain that was fastened around his waist. After his initial shock in recognizing the apparition as Jacob Marley, Scrooge had learned the meaning of all the cashboxes, keys, ledgers, padlocks, property deeds, and heavy purses attached to the chain, Marley wore. There was no shock this time, only surprise.

Marley made no sound, but merely pointed to the opposite chair in front of the fireplace, into which an obedient and curious Scrooge sat. Scrooge observed the combed hair, peaked lapels on the coat, tights, and ornate boots, as he waited for Marley to speak. But Marley didn't utter a word.

What do you say to the second appearance of an apparition, even if one you know, or previously knew? "Well, you're back?" Or, "I wasn't expecting you." But Scrooge and Marley were – in Marley's case, had been – serious and somewhat dour businessmen, not programmed for small talk.

"You no longer have a chain," observed Scrooge. He said this matter-of-factly, as if Marley's visit was routine. He also noticed that Marley no longer had a pigtail, but thought best not to mention it. The missing chain seemed a more promising subject.

"I no longer wear the chain because of your good behavior, Ebenezer," said Marley. He stood up, walked to the fire, and put his two hands into the flames. "You can't imagine how good fire feels after being frozen, Ebenezer." He rubbed his hands together and clasped them behind his back, with the look on his face that awaits a question.

Scrooge, of course, had many questions, but he became confused when Marley eagerly placed his two hands into the fire. "I thought the place you were…" he hesitated. "No, it's not hot there. It's very cold," said Marley.

Scrooge thought a moment and then concluded it made sense. Since cold was the absence of heat or light, and darkness was the absence of light, then the dark side would be cold and the light would be warm. He smiled at the thought. Winter is Hell. But about the chain.

The good that Scrooge had accomplished the last twelve months, Marley explained, accrued to himself as well as to Scrooge. The chain that he had dragged through the dark world for seven years had vanished over the last twelve months link by link, cashbox by cashbox; and the much larger chain that Scrooge had been forging with even more cashboxes and ledgers had slowly evaporated into the ether. Scrooge sighed; as much as from relief and from peace of mind.

Marley patted Scrooge on the hand, as he had done many times when he was alive, and then sat down into the chair again. "Let us talk, Ebenezer, but as friends, not as business partners. I have a request to make."

"Jacob, you were a good businessman. You took what was due to you, properly, legally. You weren't a bad person. You were good," said Scrooge.

"Good? Perhaps, but Ebenezer, I did no good! That is the difference. That is what matters. You remember how old Fezziwig allowed us to have sleeping quarters under the counter in the back of his office. The very money I saved from paying no rent helped me to buy his warehouse from his wife when he died. But I bought it for far less that I should have offered her. It was a good business deal for me, but an uncharitable one also."

"It was the money I saved from having to pay no rent that allowed me to buy a third interest in the warehouse you purchased from Mrs. Fezziwig. There was nothing uncharitable in my actions," said Scrooge.

"But we considered it only good business to force Mrs. Fezziwig from their chambers above his office that they had lived in all their life." said Marley.

"Well, Jacob, we were young, inexperienced and had little money left after purchasing the warehouse. Where is the line between proper and abusive business practices?" asked Scrooge.

"In the heart, Ebenezer, not the mind."

"Certainly our youth excused such unfeeling actions."

"Forgives but doesn't forget."

"Our sign. Do you remember the sign we ordered?" asked Scrooge. We told the painter it was to read "Marley and Scrooge" but he made a mistake and painted "Scrooge and Marley."

"I remember well our first thoughts. How I have paid over them over the years." Marley said, as an afterthought. "We saw a profit in the mistake immediately. I told the painter that we would not accept the incorrect sign. Three days later, you went to his shop and asked how much he wanted for the 'useless' sign. Glad to get rid of it, he said, "Ten pounds.""

"Half its original price!" said Scrooge.

"And that was why your name was first," said Marley.

They recalled many ventures that, while almost always legal, crossed the line between ethical and not ethical or in their words, "good business" and like the young man who tells his mother about the cookies he "borrowed" when he was a toddler, a few seemed forgivable, perhaps even humorous. They knew, of course, those for which they each had paid a high price.

Scrooge sensed that this visit was not for his own benefit, but had something to do with Marley himself. "You said something about a request, Jacob. Is there something I can do for you?"

Marley explained. He no longer existed in darkness. And through the good works of Scrooge, had come into the shadows. The chain he had worn for seven years was gone, except for four links. In Marley's world of shadows, Scrooge could be an agent for him, and what Marley needed to accomplish, but could not by himself, Scrooge could. If these four links became detached from his belt, Marley would leave the world of shadows and enter the world of Light. Would Scrooge do this?

Without hesitation, Scrooge welcomed the chance to be the instrument for whatever Marley required of him. Marley bent over, once again patted Scrooge's hand, and then pointed to the fire.

Scrooge saw a dark room in which a woman held a small child in her arms. He heard her say, "I am leaving you and taking the baby with me. It is one thing to desert me in your obsession for money, but another when it comes to our son." She turned, and slammed the door behind her. The man, to whom she was talking, returned to his desk and continued to write.

"I was that man, Ebenezer, after I had left Fezziwig and before you became my partner. The child is my son, Edward. He was raised to despise me, knowing me only as a scoundrel. Just as I have sat by you invisible many a day, Ebenezer, so I have sat by him many days these past seven years. How much I have missed that is good, loving, caring in his life. I've grown to love him. He has a shop in Saint Albans. Go there, Ebenezer, and in any way you possibly can, assure him that, his father loved him. I shall return at the same time next week."

Marley vanished. Scrooge closed his eyes, as the flames became embers.

It took Scrooge a full day to reach Saint Albans the following Wednesday and another day to return. The first person Scrooge had asked directed him to Edward Marley's bakery. The shop was small but inviting, and the aroma of Danish pastries, French tarts, German strudel, and English scones enticed Scrooge to choose one of each to complete a dozen. The strudel looked so delicious that Scrooge asked the young girl not to put it in the box, but hand it to him.

"Will there be anything else, Sir?" she asked, handing him the box.

Swallowing his first bite, Scrooge asked if Edward Marley was there, for he would like to speak with him. Swallowing and talking simultaneously, caused his words to sound like children's gibberish. With five small siblings at home, the young girl easily deciphered his words and said, she would get her father for him.

Her father? She must be Jacob's granddaughter! Does Jacob know that? Scrooge took the second and last bite. He thought it would be fun to tell Jacob, "I met your lovely granddaughter!" He thought about enjoying another strudel, when the girl came back from the bakery into the shop with a middle-aged man and pointed to Scrooge.

Edward Marley stopped at the door, brushed the flour on his hands against the large apron about his waist, and stared at the "kindly old gentleman who likes strudel" standing in front of the trays of warm Bauernbrot.

"What can I do for you?" asked the man.

"You are Edward Marley?" asked Scrooge.

"Yes. This is my bakery," he replied.

A fine figure of a man, firm narrow lips, searching eyes, Edward Marley impressed Scrooge as a fine son for Jacob. Or he would have been, had things been different. A few comments about his delicious pastries – especially the strudel – before finally asking him, if he knew or was related to Jacob Marley.

That was his father's name. Yes, he believed his father had a business near Westminster in London. He confessed that he was too young to remember when his mother took him and left his father. Hard times had made her a bitter woman and she blamed all her misfortune on his father. "As I've grown older, I've often wondered if my father ever thought about me," said Edward.

"I was a partner to your father, Edward. He died eight years ago. He thought of you much and in his imagination would visit you. He asked me to someday find you and tell you that he loved you."

"I always felt that he did." said Edward. A tear rolled down his cheek. "Please come with me in the back where we can talk further." The two young boys cleaning trays and bowls were told to "go help your sister." He pointed to a stool next to several trays of fresh dark bread, hard rolls, and one full tray of scones. Scrooge sat on the stool and savored the hot-from-the-oven aroma of the scones.

Scrooge answered Edward's questions about his father from the point of view of the last several years rather than before. He was, therefore, able to honestly describe a good and virtuous Jacob Marley, without mentioning the uniqueness of Jacob's present condition or even hinting at his earlier life. Before Edward would let Scrooge depart, he gave him a box of scones, a box of chocolate éclairs, and a box with a quarter slice of cheesecake covered with sliced peaches.

Edward's daughter wrapped the four boxes – the three Edward had given him and the one Scrooge had purchased – as two, for ease of carrying. Scrooge carefully placed the boxes on the front seat of the carriage he hired – in case of a sudden stop – and sat on the opposite seat. He indulged himself by taking one more strudel. The continual shaking of the carriage in going over the cobblestone streets invigorated Scrooge's old body. Enjoying the view of London and finishing the strudel, it struck Scrooge that this link Marley would wish to polish and retain.

Scrooge had given Bob Cratchet two boxes of the pastries and eaten the rest himself, except for one blueberry tart, which, he wanted to show to Jacob – a sample of his son's work. He thought "show" rather than "give," as he felt sure that Jacob did not and could not eat. He had placed the tart on a plate by the fireplace on the seventh evening, and waited for Marley's appearance.

The fire suddenly blazed and Marley appeared, lounging in the chair next to Scrooge. "You did very well, Ebenezer. I was by your side the entire two days you were away. Thank you. I'm pleased that you approve of Arabella." Marley smiled at Scrooge's sudden quizzical expression. "Edward's oldest child," he said. "There are five more."

"He knew!" thought Scrooge. "But why 'Edward's' rather than 'my granddaughter?'"

"You're right Ebenezer. That is the benefit of coming out of the darkness. One can reason again, for if these six are my son's children, then they are my grandchildren. I have six grandchildren! Thank you again, Ebenezer. I shall polish that link and arrange to have it transmuted into gold. I'll take my blueberry tart now."

Skeptically, Scrooge handed Marley the plate with the stale blueberry tart on it. To Scrooge' surprise, Marley took several bites – almost half – savoring each flake and berry. To his astonishment,

Scrooge watched the tart being swallowed and slowing slide down Marley's esophagus.

"Do you remember Sidney Bockingham, Ebenezer?" asked Marley.

"Yes. You had some business arrangement with him, as I remember. He committed suicide," said Scrooge.

"He hanged himself. I had loaned him money on his home for some foreign business venture he had begun. Things had not worked out as he had hoped, and he asked for extension on repayment. I was in my legal rights and refused. With the loss of his home and the failure of the business venture, he took his life."

"You weren't responsible for his death, Jacob," said Scrooge.

"Not directly. Compassion would have allowed an extension. He has a daughter. She lives near Ludgate in poor conditions. I want you to visit her and provide her with some funds from my estate." Scrooge raised his eyebrows. "Yes, I know. It was probated years ago, and belongs to you now, but, believe me Ebenezer; this will benefit you as well as me." Scrooge nodded his head in agreement.

Two days later, Scrooge went to the address near Ludgate that Marley gave him, knocked on the door, and asked the young woman who answered it, if she was Frances Crammer. Thin, hair uncombed, a dirty smock her only covering, she responded only with a nod. A second nod confirmed that her father was Sidney Bockingham. Scrooge's request to come in was answered, by opening the door half way and pointing to the one chair at the cluttered table that did not have something piled upon it, on which Scrooge sat.

Scrooge surmised from the needles and pins fastened to pieces of cloth scattered over the table, that Frances Crammer was a seamstress. A wooden crucifix hung on the back wall in front of a small table, on which sat a large silver candlestick, with a stub of an unlit candle. The two dirty cups and plates suggested that two people had eaten breakfast. A husband? A child? Scrooge began:

"Mrs. Crammer, I'm Ebenezer Scrooge. Of Scrooge and Marley. It recently came to my attention that a sum of money due your father had never been forwarded to him." This was the better approach. No need to mention details. "It is my understanding that your father is no longer living."

"Hanged himself, he did," said Frances Crammer.

Scrooge did not wish to pursue the subject. "I'm pleased to give you this money that was due to your father."

She took the check and looked at the amount. She yelled into the adjoining room. "Mum, come here!"

An old disfigured woman, bent over, dragging her left foot, came into the doorway. "Money! A great deal!" said Frances. The two women began laughing. Scrooge moved to the door, tipped his hat, and walked out onto the street. Would they be better off? He wondered.

Scrooge sensed Marley's presence when he unlocked the door to his chambers. He felt it, or rather, felt him. From the time they had first met, working at the same desk at Fezziwig's office, their singular interest – money – had guaranteed their being friends, not social, but decidedly business friends, and business partners became a natural consequence. This most recently encountered side of Marley – his spirit side – provided Scrooge not only a more challenging view of Jacob, but also of himself. Scrooge had discovered his own self, for the first time.

Scrooge looked around the room and even took a candle into his bedchamber, where the shadows danced high above on its twelve-foot high ceiling. Finally, he yelled, "Marley! Where are you?"

"Here!" replied Marley. Scrooge looked in the direction of the voice, in a corner opposite the fireplace, near the ceiling. Marley took steps down an unseen staircase and then patted Scrooge gently on his hand. "I've been waiting for you. She's insane, you know."

"The mother," said Scrooge.

"No, the daughter," replied Marley. "I have one link less, but we may have been too late."

"They were both laughing when I left, Jacob."

"But each for different reasons," said Marley. He motioned with his hand for Scrooge to sit down. "That is no longer our concern. We have done what we should have done. We both gained from your actions, Ebenezer."

Marley unhooked one of the two links still attached to his belt. He handed it to Scrooge. The link was blood red. Scrooge handed it back to Marley, who shook his head, "no." "It is for you to keep as a reminder, Ebenezer."

"A reminder of what, Jacob?" asked Scrooge.

"Listen to what I tell you and then you will know," replied Marley, and he began to explain himself once more.

Marley had been shrewd and cunning in his business dealings and had profited well from each "without crossing the line" – although sometimes it was on the line. Occasionally, the line was legal, sometimes ethical, and sometimes both. Compassion, consideration, forgiveness had not been part of Marley's business vocabulary; and since all his time and activity had centered on business, they had not been part of his life. His business acumen had warned him from charlatans, con artists, and swindlers. A man of many accomplishments and no faults. Until he met Nicholas Peel.

That Peel was a man of great wealth was obvious to Marley. That he seemed naïve encouraged Marley to plan to acquire some of this wealth for himself. Peel said the fortune to be made from his South India enterprise required only ten thousand pounds to "bring it off." Could Marley find him such an investor? Of course! Marley could not have planned better.

Marley's ten thousand became thirty thousand, but Peel suddenly left the country. All that was left of the venture was the paper he held. Peel had cheated Marley out of a small fortune.

The many links on Marley's chain had been the result of injustices he had committed, but he had committed no wrong against Nicholas Peel, and any link would have belonged to Peel. The loss of the money had not caused Marley any serious financial problems, and even the shock to his pride – a man of cunning and sly business perception being hoodwinked – soon vanished, after several "clever business deals."

But Marley had never been able to forgive Peel any minute of any working day, and since Marley worked every day, he had never forgiven Peel to his dying day. That is why the link was red. Unforgiving is not blue or green, but red, blood red. With his last breath, Marley still cursed Peel.

One dark year permits a vast amount of introspection, and Marley's seven years produced significant change within him. "Ebenezer, I have forgiven Nicholas Peel many times during these last seven years in my heart. Find him and let him know," Marley said, and then he turned around and walked up the same stairs, through the ceiling and out into the cold night air.

Marley's unusual appearances and exits – unusual from the physical point of view – no longer surprised Scrooge, who now pondered how he might locate Nicholas Peel and whether he was still alive.

The following Sunday Scrooge had dinner at his nephew's home and was introduced to Fred's partner, Rubert Walpole and his wife. Both Kathleen and Mrs. Walpole gladly included Scrooge in their conversation, for he was of the age when a man is no threat to young women. Fred and Rubert's conversation revolved around business, which did not interest Scrooge, and what aged man cannot appreciate being near pretty, young women, even to listen to them chatter?

Peel! Scrooge heard Fred say the name. Nicholas Peel! "Nephew! Did you say Peel? Would that be Nicholas Peel?"

Fred told Scrooge that he was handling the case against a Nicholas Peel, who had returned from Europe and was being sued for fraud. Peel was apparently very ill and his testimony was taken in a deposition.

Delighted with this information, Scrooge said it was time for an old man to be going home. Both couples stood up. Scrooge took the hand of Kathleen and kissed it, thanking her for inviting him. Fred was surprised by the several, "Thank you, Fred; thank you, thank you!" and would have been puzzled by his uncle's thought, "You really get things done, Jacob!"

Scrooge went to the poor house, where an attendant took him to a corner of a foul smelling hall where old men and women mumbled, yelled, chanted, cried, gyrated, and sat motionless, like the man to whom the attendant pointed. In his prime, this old man must have weighed twice the weight of this shriveled old body that stared through blind, mucous-stained eyes into space.

"Mr. Peel? Mr. Nicholas Peel?" asked Scrooge. The attendant pointed to his own eyes and ears and shook his head.

This is where man's vanity leads, thought Scrooge. He stepped close to Peel, who made no response to Scrooge's hand waving in front of him. "Mr. Peel," Scrooge whispered in Peel's ear. "I've come from Jacob Marley. You and he did a business deal many years ago. Mr. Marley lost a great deal of money, for which he held you responsible. For years, he hated you. He no longer does. He forgives you for what you took from him, and he asks you to forgive him, for his hatred of many years toward you."

Scrooge stepped back. The body of Nicholas Peel remained in its vegetative state, giving Scrooge no sign to indicate having heard his words. The attendant shrugged his shoulder. Scrooge looked into those crusty sockets, where two blurred eyes gazed into nothing and noticed a single tear slide down the right cheek and curve around the mouth, just below the lower lip. He nodded to the attendant and walked to the door, satisfied that he had done what Jacob had asked.

Jacob had mentioned four links, four tasks for Scrooge. "What will the fourth and last require of me?" thought Scrooge, as he walked toward the "Cat and Fiddle" pub. Alfred took his hat and coat and showed Scrooge his regular booth. "Is something wrong, Sir?" asked Alfred. Scrooge stood motionless, his eyes staring at the opposite side of the booth.

"Jacob!" whispered Scrooge. His exclamation was not from surprise but displeasure. Marley's "coming and going" between them was acceptable, but among others it was not, as far as Scrooge was concerned.

"I beg your pardon, Mr. Scrooge," said Alfred. "Are you all right?" He took Scrooge's hat and coat.

Scrooge sat down. "I'm all right, Alfred. The usual, please. You might bring me an ale tonight, Alfred."

Alfred left Scrooge, speculating whether the two unusual occurrences – Scrooge's behavior and his ordering ale – were connected?

Scrooge continued looking at Marley, who sat in the opposite booth, and, with only his eyes, conveyed his displeasure over Marley's appearance here and now.

"I'm sorry if I have displeased you, Ebenezer. It's cold outside and so are your chambers. Only you perceive me, so relax. Enjoy your ale! This is something new for you?"

Scrooge nodded. The events of the last few weeks justified a glass of ale. He wondered how Jacob could be bothered by such small temperature changes as experienced on earth, but decided that it was better to leave it stand by itself. To the point, he wanted to tell Jacob about Nicholas Peel, if he already didn't know, and discover what venture lay within the fourth link.

"The warmer the heart, Ebenezer, the more sensitive to cold," said Marley, answering Scrooge's first thought. "I was there. It was a real tear, Ebenezer, but Peel saw me, not you. He knows he will die in three days. I've offered to show him around. His suffering has allowed him to become a friend, Ebenezer." Scrooge's second thought was answered.

Scrooge waited, but Jacob said nothing more. His food in front of him, Scrooge ate and drank, and still waited. With the last sip of ale, Scrooge said, "Well? Are you going to tell me about the fourth link?" Alfred came to the table just as Scrooge finished speaking.

"What can I tell you, Mr. Scrooge?" asked Alfred.

"I wasn't talking to you, Alfred. Please get my hat and coat." Alfred went to get Scrooge's hat and coat, while Scrooge's eyes again showed displeasure. "Now see what you've done, Jacob. Alfred will think I'm an addle-pated old fool."

But Alfred felt kindly to Scrooge and thought, "An aging, old gentleman, bless 'im."

Marley told Scrooge, as they walked together to Scrooge's chambers, that he would tell him about the fourth link, but not go home with him tonight, as he had other things that needed to be done. Scrooge was to look in the large cabinet in his storage room, on the top shelf, behind candlesticks, vases, and other things Marley had accumulated over the years and with which Scrooge never bothered. Scrooge would find a French clock of gilded bronze with a statue of Venus next to a golden urn, which had rotating hands instead of a dial.

The clock had belonged to the grandfather of Geoffrey Ledwidge and had been sold for financial reasons. Years later, the clock was auctioned and Marley outbid Ledwidge, because he disliked Ledwidge's arrogance. Scrooge was to give the clock to Ledwidge. Marley finished, as they reached Scrooge's door. He pointed to the doorknocker. "It all began there, Ebenezer," he said, and vanished.

Scrooge paid young Wat Owen, the greengrocer's son, several shillings to help cover and carry the clock. Scrooge had found the address of Ledwidge Funds and discovered that Geoffrey Ledwidge had become a wealthy man, since the incident with the clock. He wondered if it would mean anything now to Ledwidge. He covered the clock with one of his pillowcases and let Wat carry it, while they took a cab to Ledwidge Funds.

Scrooge and Wat had to talk to three people, before being ushered into the office of Geoffrey Ledwidge. "They tell me you have something that is mine," said Ledwidge.

Scrooge and Wat placed the clock on a table in front of Ledwidge's desk and removed the pillowcase. Ledwidge stood up. "The Venus!" he exclaimed. He walked around his desk and touched the clock, moving his fingers down the back of the Venus figure. "My grandfather told me someday he would give me 'my Venus.' But he had to sell it and everything he had. Years later I discovered it was up for bid, but some scoundrel, who knew how much I wanted the clock, outbid me."

"That scoundrel returns it to you with his best wishes," said Scrooge.

"You?"

"Oh, no! I'm merely his agent."

"How much does he want?"

"Nothing. It's his gift to you."

"He wants nothing?"

"He wants only to hold the last link in his hand," replied Scrooge. He shook the hand of a perplexed but overjoyed Geoffrey Ledwidge and left with young Wat.

That night, the knocker on Scrooge's door began to pound heavily. He could not recall ever hearing the knocker before, for in truth, Scrooge never had visitors. That is, human visitors. He picked up his candle, put on a robe, and went downstairs. He slid the chain lock so that he could open the door a slight bit.

"Come, come, Ebenezer, I could as easily walk through your door, so the least you can do is open it all the way," said Marley. Scrooge didn't. He had not been pleased with the abrupt and unusual manner of Jacob's appearances these last weeks and now thought Jacob's knocking at the door far more acceptable. "Very well, Ebenezer. At the door from now on." Scrooge unlatched the chain and opened the door.

Marley told Scrooge that Ledwidge had been like a child with his new toy and had invited his entire staff to come see "his Venus." Marley couldn't believe an old family clock could bring a man so much happiness. Scrooge became concerned when Jacob mentioned that he probably could have made an excellent profit on his investment, had Scrooge offered it for sale rather than a gift. He felt more assured when Jacob added that money was of little value to him now, but the pleasure in giving was priceless. Marley looked at the clock on Scrooge's mantel.

"It was my mother's," said Scrooge, "and it's not for sale."

"I have a most important request," said Marley.

"There are more links?" asked Scrooge.

"No," said Marley, "thanks to you, my good friend. This is a different request. You must promise not to ask any questions, but do just as I bid you."

"Well, I have so far, Jacob. If what I have done these last few weeks has benefited you, it has also enlightened me," said Scrooge.

"More than benefit, Ebenezer. I have come from darkness to the shadows. What I will request from you now will bring me from the shadows to the Light."

"Tell me what I am to do, Jacob," Scrooge said forthrightly.

III

To come from darkness into the shadows and wait movement into light, conjures Western myths of hell, purgatory, and heaven, places outside one's inner-self rather than conditions within. Marley's narrations to Scrooge conveyed this awareness of "outside-ness," but upon reflection, Scrooge sensed something different occurring, not fully discerned by seeing or hearing, not sensed, but, nevertheless, a subtle awakening to a deeper truth: Scrooge and Marley were no longer Scrooge and Marley.

Bob Cratchet, Alfred, Mr. Owen the greengrocer, Nettie Straw the charwoman, Mrs. Dilbert the laundress, Charlotte Cope (who served him breakfast), all who in one way or the other served Scrooge, knew that the Mr. Scrooge of the past years was not this Mr. Scrooge. Their outward kind acts and his inward new found joy, assured Scrooge that he was no longer what he had been and convinced him that he and Marley had not just changed, like the cocooned caterpillar, but had transformed, like the emerging butterfly.

Earlier Scrooge had assumed that the change within him created the joy and happiness he felt, but now it occurred to him that the joy and happiness he allowed himself to feel, have caused the change. Is a dog happy because it wags its tail, or does it wag its tail because it is happy? Both, Scrooge would have answered.

Scrooge always heard Marley, but now he would listen to him, not with the expectations of cautious refusal of his former self, but with the willing acceptance of his new awareness. He must not question Marley about this request, neither verbally or silently within his own thoughts. This request differed from Scrooge's good efforts in removing the links, as opening a gold vault differs from opening a cell door.

"Yes, Jacob, yes! Tell me what I am to do!" Scrooge eagerly said to his friend.

Marley reached over and patted Scrooge on the back of the hand, then leaned back into the consoling wings of the chair.

"You must arrange for your nephew Fred and his wife Kathleen to be in Brighton, the tenth of July," said Marley.

Scrooge waited. This was all? One day? Why Fred? Why Kathleen? Why Brighton? No questions, Marley had said. A seemingly simple, innocuous request, not mysterious but humorous. Scrooge leaned back into his chair and sighed. A smile and a nod. Marley had expected nothing else. He stood up and raised three fingers. "We will not speak again for three weeks, Ebenezer. I have a great enterprise ahead." The door opened and Marley departed from Scrooge's chambers.

What at first seemed rather a simple thing to accomplish – that Fred and Kathleen should be in Brighton for one day, July tenth to be exact – soon presented Scrooge with far more questions than answers. Was this for the good of Fred and Kathleen or for Fred alone? Was it to protect them both, possibly to have them away from their house during a certain time? Could it be for Jacob's good? Scrooge settled at the present on his first thought that it was for their good.

Scrooge could not just tell Fred that he should take Kathleen to Brighton. "Why?" Fred would certainly ask. The reason had to be important, one that touched Fred and Kathleen. Then Fred's next question would surely be, "Why Brighton?" This was less difficult, thought Scrooge, for Brighton was one of the most popular seaside resorts in England.

Brighton! He and his sister Fanny had been invited by their Uncle Percy and Aunt Erma to go with them to Brighton that summer, the summer Ebenezer had been permitted to go home. That was nearly fifty years ago, when he was twelve and Fanny was nine. How they enjoyed those days at Brighton.

Brighton, until the 18th century, had been the small village of Brightehelmston, but then the Prince of Wales, who became George IV in 1820, found the village a good place to escape his London creditors and relax with Mrs. Fitzherbert. The Prince had the architect, John Nash, design a pavilion, an Eastern blend of onion domes and Eastern spire, to face the seafront. Young Ebenezer thought it an oriental nightmare, but Fanny, sweet Fanny, being caught up in Coleridge's poem Xanadu, said she thought the pavilion's crescents and squares to be "a stately pleasure dome."

Slipping into the reverie of old age, Scrooge recalled Fanny's wish that day on the beach at Brighton when time had vanished and happiness had encompassed them both. In Fanny's young heart, the beach at Brighton had become this timeless happiness. "Ebenezer, let us promise to return to this joyful place when we are grown up!" exclaimed Fanny.

"If that would please you Fanny, yes," said Ebenezer.

"It does please me much, Ebenezer. Our own special occasion, our own jubilation," said Fanny.

She died too young. At least Fred remembered her. Scrooge's thought meandered through visions of Fanny during her remaining twenty years. The last impinged on Scrooge's intuition so that he saw Fanny wave to him and shout, "It's our Jubilee!"

Jubilee—a celebration after fifty years. It would be fifty years this very summer, thought Scrooge. In a flash, it all came together in his mind. He had promised Fanny to meet with her in Brighton in fifty years, this very June. He would fulfill his promise and be in Brighton with the closest part of Fanny that he had. Fred and Kathleen. How could they refuse?

But Marley had specifically said July, July tenth, and the jubilee would fall in June. Just as facts should not interfere with a good story, a month should not interfere with a good cause, reasoned Scrooge. Besides, July tenth was three weeks off. Jacob had said Scrooge would not see him for three weeks. He wondered if there was a connection.

"I want you and Kathleen to come with me to Brighton," said Scrooge. They had finished dinner and were enjoying the fresh fruit and cheese Scrooge had brought. Both Fred and Kathleen looked at each other to sense what the other thought, but said nothing. "On the tenth of July," added Scrooge. Fred and Kathleen still said nothing, and folded their napkins by the side of their plates. Scrooge gave them "steak but not the sizzle." Why should they go to Brighton?

Scrooge told them about the visit he and Fanny had made with their Uncle and Aunt to Brighton nearly fifty years ago, and how he had granted Fanny her wish and promised to join her in Brighton in fifty years, for their "jubilee," as Fanny called it.

"You and Kathleen are the closest kin I have to my dear Fanny. I intend to fulfill my promise to Fanny, for both of us to be again in Brighton, I physically and she, in spirit through her son and his wife. It will be fifty years the tenth of July."

"We were in Brighton for several days after our marriage. Did you know that Uncle Scrooge?" He did not. "It would be nice to recapture that time, would it not, Kathleen?" asked Fred.

"And help fulfill Uncle Scrooge's promise to your mother," added Kathleen.

"Then it's done!" said Scrooge. Further discussion would accomplish nothing. "I shall make all the arrangements, Fred, for the coach to and back from Brighton and for accommodations for July tenth and eleventh. This will be a joyous occasion in more than one way, my dears."

Scrooge had learned long ago that once the agreement was signed, the procedures should end. He thanked them for a delicious dinner, excellent company, for their assistance in fulfilling his promise, and the beginning of a wonderful trip. With that, he left, humming an old folk tune.

The next several days were busy ones for Scrooge, arranging for three passengers to travel by coach from London to Brighton and making reservations for two nights at the Hotel Savoy. The trip by coach from London to Brighton was ten hours, which, among several stops, included lunch in Ockley. The Hotel Savoy lay adjacent to the Pavilion and would give them immediate access to the sea.

The prospects of a day at the beach in Brighton with Fred and Kathleen delighted Scrooge and he decided he would buy himself a fine new cane to take with him. He had no need for one physically, but carrying one, he believed, gave a certain distinction to an older gentleman, not unlike a soldier's medals or the scars of a young boy who wins a hard fought fight. He settled on a fine wooden cane with a silver-headed eagle.

Scrooge placed his new cane in the ceramic umbrella stand next to the door, when he returned to his chambers. Emblazoned with red Chinese dragons, the stand and the one umbrella in it had both belonged to Marley. Although Scrooge had used the umbrella many times during the last seven years, it was not until then that he noticed how common the handle was – wood painted black. Was this not a good description of his past life? The Chinese dragons deserved to be filled with a silver headed eagle, for hadn't he soared high into the sky? Well, at least his soul had.

The two chairs in front of the fireplace had been turned around during the hot summer days, and Scrooge sat down with a book about this history of Sussex County and Brighton. The umbrella stand stood fifteen feet in front of Scrooge's view, when he lifted his eyes from the pages of the book. In the deep recesses of Scrooge's primordial soul, the dragons, eagle, and silver awakened an unconscious awareness of their ancient meanings.

The Eastern dragon is the spirit of change and the eagle; spirit itself, while silver is purity. The purity of Scrooge's spiritual journey was beset by change. He closed the book and let it slip from his lap. Something had changed. What was it? The great awakening he had experienced that wonderful Christmas Eve seemed like the hot meal one savors, only to find it cold. Brighton would be the jewel in the crown of all those he had learned to love, those he saw almost every day.

Each of the spirits that had visited Scrooge that special Christmas Eve could ask now, "Have you found happiness, Ebenezer?"

Scrooge would reply, "Oh, yes, yes, but... something is missing."

Marley? No. Not Marley himself – or, more correctly, his spirit self. But maybe Marley's world! Scrooge's change of behavior had anchored him solidly in the everyday world, and that special Christmas Eve enabled him to reach toward the sky, the spiritual world that Marley came from. When you are tired, you do not lift your feet off the earth, but tired arms easily come down from their raised position. His feet were solid, but his arms had relaxed. That is what had changed. Our inner and outer selves are not two, but two halves.

Knowing is half the answer, and Scrooge felt the warmth of that Christmas Eve again begin to caress him in gentle arms of love. For the Cratchets, it was church, and for Fred and Kathleen, it was the love they had for each other. He drew the drapes and thrust open the shutters and realized that night was as beautiful as morning. For an old man he could still stretch.

They left London early on the tenth of July, struck by the sudden change from bristling London to pastoral Surrey. The southern counties were celebrated by generations of English writers as "that part of England which is properly called her Eden." By late noon, they had reached Ockley, where they stopped for lunch at the King's Arms.

Ockley seemed completely unplanned, its streets running haphazardly. Each house was a unique construction, some made of stone, others of brick or flint, some thatched, others tiled. It was here, Scrooge explained to Kathleen, on the village green, with its great width still visible, that Ethelwulf, the ruler of Wessex, defeated the Danes in 851. Leith Hill could be seen through the window next to their table. Fred mentioned that some historians alleged that the famous battle took place there. Scrooge decided that he needed a more modern history book.

By late evening, they reached Brighton. In recent years as the middle class flocked to "London by the Sea," royalty left. Queen Victoria found the pavilion too public, but Brighton continued to display it. After registering at the Hotel Savoy, Scrooge insisted that Fred and Kathleen tour the pavilion where the Music Room was decorated in "Chinese Gothic" with writhing silver dragons, iron palms, and a one-ton chandelier.

Scrooge had reserved a table that evening for supper. Fred and Kathleen followed the maître d'hôtel to their table, while Scrooge stopped to talk to two gentlemen with whom he had done business several years ago. They acknowledged him as Mr. Scrooge initially, but with his emergence as the "new Scrooge," they exclaimed, "Good to have seen you, Ebenezer," as he left to join Fred and Kathleen.

Scrooge walked to the empty chair to the right of Fred and opposite Kathleen. Someone was sitting in the fourth chair? It was Marley.

Marley placed his finger to his lips. Scrooge slowly sat down as the waiter pulled his chair out from the table.

"Are you all right, Uncle?" asked Fred. Marley smiled. Scrooge replied, "Yes."

Brighton was not turning out to Scrooge's satisfaction. He certainly did not expect to see Marley in Brighton. Marley had said that they would not speak for three weeks, but Scrooge heard "see." Also Marley said he had business to attend to – some great enterprise – but did not mention where. Now he sees Marley sitting at their table, putting his finger to his lips so Scrooge would not speak to him. He also found Marley's hovering over Kathleen irritating. The entire situation disturbed Scrooge.

Fred and Kathleen, on the other hand, celebrated a second honeymoon, holding hands, laughing at Fred's stories, and toasting "Good, old Uncle Scrooge." Marley joined in the toast – ambrosian mist in an ethereal glass – and merely shook his head sadly, when Scrooge excused himself. Seeing Marley, but not talking with him, was different from talking with him, but not seeing him. One can comfortably speak to an unseen God, but discomfort arises in seeing God, but not being able to speak, vocally or within.

"See you at breakfast, children," said Scrooge. Then he left.

Looking like newlyweds, Fred and Kathleen welcomed Scrooge to breakfast. Marley was there; his finger again up to his lips. They would meet Scrooge for lunch after visiting all the stores in Brighton. Scrooge handed Kathleen a number of pounds. "Do more than shop, my dear. Buy something beautiful for yourself," said Scrooge. Marley jumped up to pull Kathleen's chair back and then sauntered off with her and Fred. He again held his finger to his lips and raised three fingers toward Scrooge.

Scrooge had found the large rock that he and Fanny had sat on those many years ago when he made his promise to her. The gulls still encouraged visitors to feed them, and beachcombers continued to gather seashells. The setting had not changed, but he and Fanny, actors upon this coastal stage, had.

A child on the other side of the rock called out "Mommy, Mommy!" to a figure walking along the shore. The woman turned and waved. She looked like Fanny the last time Scrooge had seen her. She began running to the rock, waving frantically, as the child continued to yell, "Mommy, Mommy!" The closer she came, the younger she became, until Scrooge whispered, "It is Fanny." By the time she was within speaking distance, she became the Fanny who had sat on this rock fifty years ago.

Scrooge reached out, but before he could grasp her hands, she vanished, and where the small child had stood, a gull flapped its wet wings.

Fred and Kathleen had lunch and supper with Scrooge, who also had lunch and supper at the same time with Marley, the Quiet, as Scrooge styled him. "Marley has much to explain tomorrow," Scrooge mulled to himself, "when these 'three weeks of silence' will have ended."

Marley sat atop the luggage piled on the roof of the coach. Scrooge appreciated Marley's good judgment by not attempting to sit in the full coach; although, in his non-material state, he would require no space. Even during the several stops, Marley remained atop the coach; but when they arrived that evening in London and transferred to a carriage, Marley sat in the carriage next to Scrooge.

The carriage stopped first at Fred and Kathleen's home. Kathleen leaned over and kissed Scrooge on the cheek, as she stepped down from the carriage, both she and Fred thanked him for a wonderful two days. They waved even after the carriage left their house. Scrooge, on the other hand, turned his attention to Marley, glad that it had not been necessary to prevent Marley from going with Fred and Kathleen.

"Well?" said Scrooge.

Marley patted Scrooge on the hand. "We may talk now, Ebenezer. The three weeks have past. My great enterprise has proved most successful."

"I have done exactly as you requested, Jacob. Am I not entitled to explanations, reasons, clarification?"

"Indeed you are. When we arrive at your chambers."

When they arrived at Scrooge's chambers, Scrooge immediately began to question Marley.

"Now, Jacob. Now. Why did Fred and Kathleen need to be in Brighton on the tenth? Why were you there? What is this great enterprise?" asked Scrooge.

"Ebenezer, Kathleen is with child!" Scrooge became silent. "Had she remained in London on the tenth, a tramp soul would have entered the child. Conditions in Brighton on the tenth allowed for – shall I say – an old soul, one journeying on the spiritual path, to claim the child."

A year ago, Scrooge would have had great difficulty assimilating what Marley was telling him with any reasonable chance of understanding. His encounters with Marley these past months had conditioned his reasoning to accept "the unacceptable," what is normally not "reasonable," but he intuitively grasped the unique situation that parents make babies not souls.

"An old soul, you say?" asked Scrooge.

"Yes. Me!" exclaimed Marley.

IV

Marley stood in front of the fireplace with his hands extended behind himself. Scrooge removed his hat, scarf, and topcoat and stared at Marley. "There is much you must explain," he said.

"There is much you must learn," replied Marley.

Annoyed by Marley's complacency, Scrooge needed to find some vulnerable spot in Marley's behavior. "What are you doing with your hands in the fireplace?"

"Warming them, of course," replied Marley, intentionally self-contented.

"There is no fire in the fireplace, Marley." Calling him "Marley" rather than "Jacob" indicated the change of an informal to formal relationship.

Marley turned around and looked at the fireplace. "By Harry, you are right, Scrooge." The change from "Ebenezer" to "Scrooge" was intentional, but in humor, not ill will. Marley reached out to Scrooge and placed his arm about his shoulder. "Ebenezer, please. Sit down. You have done for me more than could be expected, and I am grateful. Our journey is the same. Mine, merely a few steps ahead of yours. Everything shall be explained. You are entitled to nothing less. Come, my friend, forgive me for what I may find humorous but you, mistreatment. Make a fire for the both of us against this chill."

Nettie Straw had left a pile of dry firewood and small kindling twigs by the fireplace, and Scrooge soon had a bright fire burning. Silently, they both warmed their hands by the fire, and after a few minutes, Marley pointed to the two chairs in front of them.

Having been part of the happenings at and after Brighton, Scrooge found no problem or difficulty in the explanations Marley related. That death did not end opportunities for rectifying past mistakes appealed to Scrooge's sense of justice, for the three score years allowed a normal lifetime were much too few. Scrooge nodded affirmatively with Marley's description of a soul's return.

The returns were not random but arranged on the principle of reaping what is sown. That also met with Scrooge's approval, for it was just, and Scrooge had always felt nature at its deepest level to be just, to be balanced. Returns, like tomorrows, were gifts, opportunities to change unwelcomed habits, enhance the merging abilities, and acquire additional skills.

"We are our souls, Ebenezer, not the body we inhabit. Am I not living proof of this?" asked Marley.

Scrooge questioned Marley's use of the word "living," but Marley's presence, as phenomenon or Scrooge's personal vision, were sufficient proof that "Marley" had not ceased with the death of his body. Still Scrooge appeared skeptical, and Marley thought an example would be helpful.

"David Garrick played many Shakespearean roles on the London stage in the late 1700s, Ebenezer: Hamlet, Richard III, King Lear, and even Macbeth, as I remember, reading with Mrs. Pritchard. His acting ability was such that audiences believed he was Hamlet, or King Richard, Lear, and even Macbeth; and so immersed did he become in his role, that, had you interrupted him during the play and asked who he was, he would have said, "Hamlet," or "Richard, King of England," or "Macbeth." Yet, after the play, if you went behind stage and called out for Mr. Garrick, he would have answered."

"Then our life is a role on the stage of the world?" asked Scrooge.

"Only Shakespeare has said it better, Ebenezer."

"And like David Garrick, we play many roles on this world stage?" asked Scrooge.

"Excellent! Fortunately, previous roles are forgotten, but each return brings the habits acquired."

"Good or bad habits?" asked Scrooge.

"Both," said Marley.

"Why Brighton?" asked Scrooge.

Marley shrugged his shoulders.

"So Marley didn't know everything," thought Scrooge. That was assuring at this moment. From what Scrooge had been told so far, it appeared Kathleen had conceived a child and Marley had the opportunity to enter its body at birth. Scrooge wondered if Marley (Marley as his soul) had anything more to do.

This was another irritation for Scrooge; Marley's response to questions Scrooge had not yet articulated. "Was their conversation on the other side, or was there only continuous nodding of heads?" wondered Scrooge.

"Do you wish answers to both questions?" asked Marley.

"What do you mean?" replied Scrooge.

"Do I converse with my fellow soul mates, and what else I must do before assuming the role of the child Kathleen will deliver?" replied Marley. The last question formed in Scrooge's mind at the same time Marley stated it.

"Both," was Scrooge's challenge.

"We converse by thought but perceive as sound." Since this seemed to satisfy Scrooge, Marley continued. "I must be around Kathleen during this period, like a person who watches his house being built. I can suggest to the builder possible changes, additions, eliminations – suggestions that I can afford, that is that I have a right to suggest. The builder in this case, is the 'great mother source' creating the child."

"What about her and Fred's privacy?" asked Scrooge.

Marley raised his hands. "Nothing can enter the private sanctum of an individual, unless permitted. Fred and Kathleen's privacy is assured, not only by degree, but by my own integrity." Marley felt a tinge of distress at the implication of Scrooge's question. Scrooge's comment "Of course," erased this physical vestige of pride that lingered with Marley.

"My dear Ebenezer, the wondrous light of truth that leads from darkness to divine light is neither bestowed casually nor embraced effortlessly, and nothing should be considered too difficult to discover that light and follow it," said Marley. "I shall be visiting Kathleen most of the time during her pregnancy. It takes patience and concentration to adjust to the small body.

I must be there when he is born, you understand, when he takes that first breath."

"Kathleen is going to have a boy?" asked Scrooge.

"Yes, of course. I am and was quite comfortable as a man and have no reason to change," replied Marley.

"Then you have a choice?" asked Scrooge.

"If you've earned it," answered Marley. "You helped me earn it. We've been helping each other, as we did in our business."

"Don't mention our business. That's why you visited me seven years ago," said Scrooge.

"There is nothing improper about business, Ebenezer. It is how you do the business that counts. We were, you are, honest in business. It was our greed, not our morals that caused us personal problems," said Marley. "Now back to the child."

"I'd like to be called Jeffery. It retains the J in my present name," said Marley. "I'll try to plant the name in Kathleen's thoughts, and maybe you can help." After all, Ebenezer, you're to become a great-uncle. I'll be your great-nephew, Ebenezer!"

"Don't you mean Jeffery – if they name him that – will be my great-nephew?"

"You're right, Ebenezer. Soon I shall change from this role as Jacob Marley to that of Jeffery Langdon. Actually, relationships exist only in the roles we play. As souls, we are not related. When the child is born, the role of Jacob Marley will have ended."

"So you're saying I wouldn't be able to talk with Jacob after the child is born?" asked Scrooge.

"You wouldn't have called David Garrick "Hamlet" when he played Lear," said Marley.

Scrooge wondered, "If David Garrick played the roles of Hamlet, Richard, Lear, and Macbeth, then who was it that played the role of Jacob and would soon play the role of Jeffery, the name hopefully bestowed on Fred and Kathleen's son?" He asked, "If I were watching Hamlet, I would speak of "Hamlet," but I would know that the player was always Garrick, the permanent name he had regardless of what character he played. " Jacob, do you have a permanent name?"

"I have one only until this Great Dream of the world ends," said Marley.

"Then you'd better tell me what it is now," said Scrooge. A

flippant response often follows difficulty in assimilating a serious idea, and Scrooge's flippant response was of this nature. Marley did not judge Scrooge's flippant manner, but reached deeper, understanding Scrooge's confusion and perplexity with "Great dream ending."

"This name cannot be spoken or written, for it would then no longer be my name."

"You seem to know a great deal about many mysterious things, Jacob," said Scrooge.

"And so do you, Ebenezer. All you need to do, all anyone needs to do for that matter, is improve the knowing deep within yourself," said Marley. "But we are too philosophical when we should be elated. My time must be spent with Kathleen, not you. But before you and I, Jacob and Ebenezer, bid each other farewell, I shall come once more to you."

"As Jacob?" asked Ebenezer.

"As Jacob," replied Marley.

V

Home only two days from her "second honeymoon" in Brighton, Kathleen had no reason to know she was with child, and of course, neither did Fred. This was not the case with Scrooge. He knew. Not only that Kathleen was to have a baby, but also that it would be a boy.

He took great delight in visualizing the tiny babe cradled in its mother's arms with its toothless gums and baldhead mimicking his grandsires, in this case a granduncle. Like lighting a new candle with the last remaining flicker of a spent one, Scrooge felt within himself an unexpected vitality of spirit, the welcomed excitement of planning a journey in the closing days of ending one, and the enjoyment of knowing what others will be thrilled to know. "Kathleen must have special attention now," thought Scrooge.

He would see to that. It would have to be subtle. He could hardly announce to Kathleen, "You're going to have a baby!" He would find some excuse to visit. To see if they have recovered from the trip? Yes. He smiled. His watch assured him that the time was appropriate; and his coat, hat, and cane assured him that his excitement would be formally hidden. He held his cane more like a baton than as means of support and began his journey of revelation.

Fred would be home by now. They would certainly invite Scrooge to dine with them. He would accept by the tone of his reply that he should not impose upon their kindness. They would insist, hearing his tone of acceptance and ignore his words, and he would then graciously accept. It would be prudent, if one contemplates an invitation to dine, to bring something to the table.

Mr. Owen, the greengrocer, had just received a large box of fresh strawberries picked that morning. Scrooge selected a dozen the size of a small hen's eggs, and asked Mr. Owen if he could wrap them fancy, in a box, with ribbon. Mrs. Owen came to Mr. Owen's rescue and presented Scrooge with a red box, filled with strawberries, tied with a golden ribbon.

Why not send some fresh strawberries to the Cratchets? This time the fresh strawberries were placed in a plain bag and tied with a string. Young Wat Owen had seen the "generous Mr. Scrooge" from the back of the shop, and ready to be of any service Mr. Scrooge might require, came out to say hello. For two shillings, he delivered the box to the Cratchets with the compliments of Mr. Ebenezer Scrooge. The one strawberry would not be missed from the bag.

The purple asters and pink wild roses had been picked from the field that morning. Yes, they were from her family farm, she told Scrooge. She placed a black-eyed Susan in Scrooge's coat lapel. "No charge, governor," she said, and winked.

The arrangement of two hands and two packages proved satisfactory, until the doorknocker needed to be rapped. Some juggling and twisting and Scrooge had a free hand. The return to two hands for two packages removed the discomfort. No one came to the door. Again, juggling and twisting, but this time the free hand remained free.

Fred opened the door and saw his Uncle Scrooge's smiling face next to a bouquet of flowers. Before Scrooge could explain his visit, Fred took the flowers in one hand and his uncle's free arm with the next, bringing both into the hall.

"Kathleen will be glad you are here, Uncle," said Fred. "She's had an accident. The doctor just left."

Scrooge followed Fred up the stairs and down the hall, to Kathleen's bedroom and heard him say that she had fallen and hurt her ankle. Why had she fallen? Was it only her ankle that was hurt? "Uncle Ebenezer is here, Kathy," said Fred. Kathleen was sitting in a chair next to her bedroom window. Next to her, on the bed, sat Marley.

"She's all right," said Marley. Scrooge's wide eyes and open mouth required another assurance. "They can't hear or see me, Ebenezer." Scrooge's eyes glowed and his lips quivered. "It would be better not talk to me," added Marley.

"Uncle Ebenezer!" cried Kathleen, holding out her hand.

"The flowers are for you," said Scrooge. He had removed his scarf and draped it over the bed, next to Marley, and held his hat in his other hand. Fred held up the bouquet for Kathleen to see, and then placed them in a vase on the table. "And look! Fresh strawberries!" He handed her the box, which she in turn, after thanking Scrooge, gave to Fred to give to the cook.

"You should have a shawl around your shoulders, Kathleen," said Scrooge.

"Why, Uncle Ebenezer, I'm quite warm," said Kathleen.

"She's perfectly all right," added Marley.

"You're no doctor," Scrooge said somewhat testily to Marley.

"Well, I'm not a doctor, but I know how I feel," said Kathleen. "Please don't concern yourself, Uncle."

"See, Ebenezer? You are well advised to say nothing more," said Marley.

"I will not!" said Scrooge.

"Don't concern yourself, Uncle," said Fred. "Kathy is in good hands with Doctor Chamberlain."

"I shall take care of Kathleen," said Marley.

"You stay out of it," Scrooge replied to Marley.

"Uncle!" said a surprised Fred.

"Oh, Fred," said Scrooge, "I wasn't talking to you."

Fred and Kathleen glanced at each other and shook their heads.

The situation had become untenable.

"I must leave," said Scrooge. "Are you coming with me?" he asked of Marley.

It was said as a question but intended as a command or at least a request.

"My duty lies here, Ebenezer," said Marley.

Fred heard only Scrooge's comment, "Are you coming with me?"

"Why, no, Uncle," he answered. "Do you need help getting home?"

Scrooge, however, answered Marley. "Don't make a nuisance of yourself."

"I only wish to help, Uncle," said Fred.

"No, Fred, I don't need any help. Take good care of Kathleen. I can leave by myself. You stay here." He managed a smile, but the last person he set eyes on was Marley.

Fred and Kathleen heard the door close. Scrooge had forgotten his scarf. Baffled by Scrooge's unusual behavior, both Fred and Kathleen sought an explanation. In moments like this, it was better for Marley to be absent. He looked at the scarf, shook his head, and walked out through the door.

"He's concerned about me," said Kathleen.

"He's getting old," said Fred.

Three days later at breakfast, Kathleen expressed concern for Scrooge and suggested that Fred stop by Scrooge's office to see how he was. On his way to his office, Fred took the longer route, which led past "Scrooge, Marley, and Cratchet." He could also see Peter Cratchet in his new accounting position.

Several months previously, Fred had mentioned to Scrooge that young Peter Cratchet, who had been working at Fred's business for some months, had a head for figures. The day before, Scrooge had told Bob Cratchet to hire someone to help him in the office. Scrooge had been spending less and less time in the office and the extra work had fallen on Bob Cratchet. The next day Scrooge, after Fred mentioned young Peter Cratchet, asked Bob if he had found anyone yet. When Cratchet said no, Scrooge said, "What about Peter?" Within a week, young Peter Cratchet sat at the work stand next to this proud father.

Bob Cratchet greeted Fred and pointed to Peter, working steadily at his work stand, and motioned for him to come and greet Mr. Langdon. Fred congratulated Peter on hearing of his engagement. Peter returned to his work stand and Fred asked when Scrooge would be in, since he observed he was not in his own office.

Scrooge had not been in for three days, which was not usual. He came every morning, but most of the time did not return after lunch, which was always at the "Cat and Fiddle." Bob assured Fred that Scrooge was in good health, alert in his work, and a pleasure to be around. He had seen no "forgetfulness" or "odd" behavior on Scrooge's part. However, Scrooge's absence of three days concerned him. It concerned Fred too.

An additional detour and Fred stood before the door to Scrooge's house. The door was locked. He raised the knocker and let it fall once. The gentleman who passed by when Fred had knocked, had now gone around the corner. This time he held the knocker and rapped several times with it.

He heard the key click and saw the knob turn. Mrs. Straw looked out of the narrow opening, which the latch permitted. Recognizing Mr. Langdon, she unchained the door and said she was glad he had come. She was concerned for poor Mr. Scrooge, sitting in his chair all day with his poor bruised foot, either resting on a stool or hurting in a washbasin of hot salt water. She had been bringing him his meals these three days, but could not get him to get in bed.

Scrooge was asleep in his chair, a nightcap on his head, and his robe tied loosely about him. His bandaged foot rested on a small stool. An accumulation of papers was stacked around his chair, and the breakfast on the tray beside him was only half consumed.

Mrs. Straw had not mentioned any injury to Scrooge's head; but a bandage that covered one eye and ear was wrapped around his head. This momentarily brought Fred memories of reading about the famous Scottish pirate Captain Kidd, whom William III had initially commissioned as a privateer, and later had hanged as a pirate.

A gentle shaking did not awaken Scrooge, but several shouts of "Uncle Scrooge! Uncle Scrooge!" did. Scrooge took time to acclimate himself to the moment, and then recognizing Fred, pointed to a chair and motioned that he move it closer and sit in it.

Mrs. Straw asked if he'd be needing anything she could bring with his lunch. His response that a new right foot would be appreciated, lightened Fred's concern; and when all three chuckled, the heavy gloom that had filled the room suddenly vanished.

Scrooge had become suddenly dizzy and fallen while walking up his stairs, after returning from Fred and Kathleen's home. He had sprained his ankle and bruised the side of his face when he fell, but managed to crawl to his chambers. The next morning Mrs. Straw found him on the floor and helped him prepare to go to bed. She had fetched Doctor Chamberlain, who bandaged Scrooge's ankle and head and told him to rest and keep his foot in hot salt water.

"Uncle Scrooge, you should come and live with Kathleen and me," said Fred. Scrooge immediately reminded Fred that he had a wife who would not necessarily appreciate an old man living in her house. That was true. Fred must first talk with Kathleen. But he was determined that his uncle should live with them. He did not continue the subject with Scrooge, for his mind was already made up. Scrooge would live with him and Kathleen.

Fred said he would stop by on the way home that evening. "Think about my suggestion, Uncle Ebenezer," was his parting words to Scrooge. That, he took, to be a sign of a more personal invitation. The problem was that Fred was going to become a father and did not know it yet. A baby and a great-uncle might be too much for Kathleen.

For the following several months, Fred and Kathleen visited Scrooge at his home. His ankle had been broken, not sprained, and healing required time and as little movement on Scrooge's part as possible. Until now, Fred had not broached the subject of Scrooge living with him and Kathleen. Certain events made this the proper time.

Doctor Chamberlain had informed Kathleen that her illness was natural; she was to have a child. Fred's rejoicing soon changed to concern for Kathleen's condition. She should sit down and rest. Would she like something to drink or eat? Can I do something for you? She answered all the questions with a smile, except the last one. He could do something for her.

Both of their parents were deceased. Their child would have no grandparents. If Uncle Ebenezer were to live with them, as Fred remarked some months before, not only would he be a continual joy to her, but a living grandparent for their child. Would he, Fred, try to persuade his uncle to come live with them? That would please her.

Fred brought Scrooge to his home in a cab, although the distance was but a few minutes' walk. Scrooge was able to walk, but Fred preferred a cab to be sure. Scrooge remembered his last visit of several months ago and his abrupt departure. He would ignore Marley. Kathleen greeted him at the door when he arrived. Certainly, the Queen could not be more welcomed.

Scrooge observed that Fred and Kathleen were as much in love as before, except that Fred was more solicitous to her than before, to which Kathleen seemed pleasingly indifferent. After dinner, they retired to the parlor. "Will they tell me that they're to have a child?"

Determined to ignore Marley, Scrooge now found himself wondering where he was. Ignoring something that isn't there is difficult to ignore.

"Have you given consideration to my suggestion of several months ago?" asked Fred.

"What suggestion was that, Fred?" asked Scrooge, although he remembered.

"That you come live with Kathleen and me."

Scrooge said nothing. He looked at Kathleen. "Two is harmony; three is not," he replied.

Scrooge remained silent, while his eyes darted between Fred and Kathleen. They were going to tell him. He must appear surprised and then pleased. He would have to pretend the surprise, but not the pleasure. He had been waiting a long time to hear from their own lips, that he was to be a great-uncle. The invitation to live with them now appeared in a different light. Kathleen wished it.

"What Kathleen means, Uncle Ebenezer," – there was that 'Uncle Ebenezer' rather than 'Uncle Scrooge' again – "is that we are going to have a baby," said Fred.

"Wonderful! A lucky child to have such parents," exclaimed Scrooge. "Congratulations to the both of you!"

"If you lived with us, Uncle Ebenezer, you'd be a comfort to me and a godfather to the child. Our child will have no living grandparents, except for you, his only grand-uncle," said Kathleen.

Scrooge asked Kathleen how she was—Excellent!—and when the child was due—early spring—but he said nothing about living with them. Fred felt this was the time to show Scrooge the two rooms in the rear of the house that would be his private chambers.

Fred led Scrooge down the hallway and opened a door opposite the kitchen. A damp smell greeted them when they entered the larger of the two adjoining rooms; but sunlight, coming through the tall windows, cast a warm glow on the sheets covering a hodgepodge of furniture. Used for storage, the rooms were seldom visited.

The larger room would be Scrooge's parlor, which Fred observed was about the size of Scrooge's present parlor. The second room was even larger than Scrooge's present bedchamber. A door from the larger room opened to a brick wall that led to the back garden, and in the opposite direction, to the street. Scrooge would be as independent as he was now and in one sense, even more so.

Scrooge visualized his own furniture arranged in the large room, and his bed, chest, and table in the smaller, but said nothing. He liked the rooms being on the first floor – no stairs to climb and the separate entrance provided him independence, as well as granting Fred and Kathleen privacy. He still said nothing, even when he and Fred returned to the parlor, where Kathleen waited.

"If Kathleen wishes it, then I wish it," said Scrooge.

"Then it's agreed!" exclaimed Fred. He filled three glasses with the Bordeaux wine he had recently purchased and gave a glass to Scrooge and Kathleen. They toasted Uncle Ebenezer, the expectant parents, the Queen, and the child that would soon grace their home.

"About your son, Fred," started Scrooge.

"It might be a girl, Uncle Ebenezer," said Fred.

Scrooge started to say, "No. It will be a boy," but realized that Marley would caution him to be discrete. He prudently said, "Of course; a boy or a girl." He placed his half-empty glass on the table. "Have you decided on a name for the child?" he asked.

They hadn't. They had, however, agreed that if the child was a girl, Fred would choose the name and if a boy, Kathleen would. Scrooge now wished Marley was around with his special "abilities" to encourage Kathleen to choose the name "Jeffrey" for their future son.

"Have you chosen a name, if it's a girl, Fred?"

"Yes, several, but I lean toward my mother's name, Fanny," said Fred.

"That would please your mother very much, Fred," said Scrooge. "And if it's a boy?" Certainly, Marley had used his special abilities by now. Scrooge would press hard this time. "Is there a boy's name, Kathleen, which stands out in your thought?"

"Yes, now that you ask, Uncle Ebenezer, my Uncle Jeffrey keeps coming to mind. He was my mother's favorite brother and certainly a wonderful uncle to me. He had no children of his own, but treated me as if I were his little girl. I was always his 'little Kathy.' Jeffery, if that meets with Fred's approval." Fred nodded his head.

Silently Scrooge said, "You're a wonder, Marley." Aloud he said, "A fine name, Kathleen. Jeffery Langdon. A name to be proud of."

Marley suddenly stepped into the room and leaned against the door, and smiled.

VI

Scrooge felt secure with his old furniture, but his new chambers, with their lower ceilings and tall windows, challenged his old habits. Sunlight replaced day candles. Warmth from a large fireplace precluded shawls, night covers, and the need for a bed-warmer. The two large windows allowed the garden to "come in" rather than Scrooge "having to go out." The evening meal was now enjoyed with company. But where was Marley?

Marley had told Scrooge that his time was to be spent with Kathleen and not him. He also said that he would come to Scrooge one more time, before they would bid each other farewell. Scrooge assumed this meant when the baby – Jeffery – was born, when Jacob, as soul, would enter the child's body. Scrooge could expect Marley to come sometime around the beginning of spring. Scrooge, however, by moving to Fred and Kathleen's home, had also "come" to Marley. Where was Marley?

Fall and winter passed and Scrooge had put Marley out of his thoughts, while he observed Kathleen become "great with child." He proved a comfort to Kathleen and a help with Fred's personal business. He retained his old routine but at a slower pace: occasional lunch at the "Cat and Fiddle," mornings at "Scrooge, Marley, and Cratchet," more frequent purchases at the greengrocer's, and joyful visits of exploration in the toy store, where Neil, the owner's son, explained some of the more complicated toys: "You put the coin here and release this lever, which propels the coin into the mouth of the clown."

It was late February when he came, and then most unexpectedly, to Scrooge. The heavy snow of the last several days had brought most of London business to a halt. The accounts at "Scrooge, Marley, and Cratchet" had fallen behind and Scrooge gladly helped bring them up to date. The noonday bells had just sounded, when a young man opened the door. Scrooge took no notice of the older gentlemen, who followed the young man into the front office. Peter Cratchet came to his office and said there was someone to see Mr. Ebenezer Scrooge.

"Who are they?" asked Scrooge.

"It's just a young gentleman, Mr. Scrooge. He has a small package with him."

"Isn't the older gentleman with him?" asked Scrooge.

"What old gentleman, Mr. Scrooge?" asked Peter.

Scrooge got up and walked to the door. It was Marley. "Come in, young man," said Scrooge. Peter left and the young man stepped into Scrooge's office. Marley followed and sat in the chair opposite Scrooge's desk. "What is it you want?" Scrooge glanced at Marley, wondering if this was the promised last visit.

"I was given two shillings to deliver this package to a Mr. Ebenezer Scrooge at "Scrooge, Marley, and Cratchet." Are you Mr. Ebenezer Scrooge?" the young man asked.

Scrooge acknowledged being himself, gave the young man a few coppers, and sat the box he was given on his desk. The young man left, but Marley remained. Scrooge decided he would wait for Marley to speak first. Carefully he opened the wrapped box and removed the top. On a white satin cushion lay a fine silver chain, the links of which were smaller than the eye of an even smaller needle.

Scrooge sat down at his desk and held the chain with the fingers of his right hand. He looked at Marley, determined not to begin the conversation.

"It's for me," said Marley.

"You?" said Scrooge.

"Well, for Jeffery. It's your gift to him. It's pure silver, Ebenezer, and the tiny clasp will enable it to be easily placed around his neck. I hope you like it," said Marley.

Scrooge placed the silver chain back into the box and fastened the lid on top. "I'm to keep it?" asked Scrooge.

"Yes, of course. It's common for children to wear a silver chain at their baptism. I like the idea, and I'm sure so will Jeffery," said Marley.

"Is this the last visit you spoke of months ago?" asked Scrooge.

"Yes. May we leave for the "Cat and Fiddle" now?" asked Marley.

Scrooge nodded his head and began putting on his coat.

His door was closed, but Bob Cratchet and Peter could hear Scrooge mumbling to himself. Bob remembered Fred Langdon asking him if he ever noticed any odd behavior in Scrooge. Had he meant something like this? When he next saw Mr. Fred, he would mention it.

Their walk to the "Cat and Fiddle" took them past the flower girl, who had pinned a flower to Scrooge's lapel the previous summer. Scrooge hadn't seen her since then. With a bunch of flowers in each hand, she walked up to Scrooge and Marley. "Will each of you kind gentlemen buy a bunch?"

Did you say "gentlemen?" asked Scrooge.

"Yes, Goveneur. You and this bloke that's dressed for summer," said the girl. "Buy my flowers?"

"Just one bunch," said Scrooge.

She returned to her stall and Scrooge looked at Marley. "I'm as surprised as you are," said Marley. "I don't know everything, Ebenezer. Where do you think she got those flowers this early in the year?"

"The same place you obtained this silver chain," said Scrooge.

"Scrooge is smarter than I imagined," thought Marley.

Their conversation at the pub was interrupted each time Alfred came to their booth. Scrooge ordered ale again (a habit that helps rejuvenate old men's blood), but he drank only half. Marley began to describe the world from which he came, but the noise prevented Scrooge from hearing most of it. He was pleased when Marley said they should go home now. Scrooge pondered the thought that it was home for both of them now and would be even more so after spring.

Alfred wondered what was in the little box.

Scrooge entered his new quarters through the outside door. Marley, who in a sense had been a resident longer than Scrooge, had merely walked through the house and was sitting in a chair in front of the fireplace, before Scrooge entered. Scrooge searched with no luck for a match to light the logs that were set in the fireplace.

"Perhaps I can help," said Marley. He rubbed his left index finger across the rough-finished side of the iron grate. He held up his hand to show Scrooge the flame at the end of his finger. The pile of logs burst instantly into flame when he touched them. Holding his finger to his lips, Marley blew out the flame and smiled at an incredulous Scrooge.

Preferring to ignore Marley's fit of showmanship, Scrooge asked about something that had been puzzling him since seeing Marley today. Marley was younger.

"And you're older," said Marley.

"I'm serious, Jacob. You appear much younger than you did the last time we spoke, and you appear to me as you did not many years after we became partners."

"I too am serious, Ebenezer. Can't you see that I must grow younger, for I shall soon be born; while you must grow older, for you will soon end your present role as Ebenezer Scrooge? It's quite logical, quite reasonable."

It wasn't for Scrooge. It was then that he decided it was better to listen to Marley, to learn as much as possible from him, while he could, while their last visit remained, and later, attempt to digest all he heard, all he could remember. Marley knew his decision, actually expected it, and continued.

"You will soon be where and what I am leaving, Ebenezer. Listen and advance many lives. At present you use all five senses to understand, but where I come from, and where you soon shall go, you shall see, hear, smell, taste, and touch only with intuitional feeling.

"You will communicate telepathically with those that join your level of understanding. As one self-redeemed, you may travel freely, while harmful entities are confined to limited zones: those levels we learned as purgatory, limbo, hell, Hades, Sheol, Gehenna, inferno, the bottomless pit, the abode of the damned.

"You will not be subject to cold or heat and other natural conditions. Remember how I warmed myself by a cold fire? Should you occasionally be cut or bruised, you will instantly heal yourself by merely willing it, and through your will, you shall dematerialize and materialize your form as you wish."

"What do I actually see when I look at you, Jacob?" asked Scrooge.

"You see subtle vibrations of light, and I am sustained by cosmic light. The physical particles that compose your body, Ebenezer, and the luminous lightrons that manifest to you as my body, are both in reality created from minute particles of thought. Thoughtrons, if you wish. What you see when you look at me is an exact counterpart of the last physical body I possessed—the Jacob Marley who was your partner.

"Soon I shall be drawn back into your terrestrial realm at a lawfully fixed time. The process will be my "death" but in shedding this luminous body form for a material one, I shall feel no pain. There is no actual pain in terrestrial death; only the loss of consciousness of flesh and the beginning awareness of one's luminous body."

"The same for everyone?" asked Scrooge.

"The amount of Light depends on the level of enlightenment. Your complete redemption enables you to avoid the shadows and enter Light, if ever so dim."

"Is there no pain, no discomfort in Light?" asked Scrooge.

"Pain is felt when there is mistake in conduct or in the perception of the truth. Physical desires are rooted in egoism and sense pleasures. When they appear, you no longer hear the ethereal music of the spheres and no longer see the exhaustless expressions of light. You begin your dream on earth."

"Will we see each other again, Jacob?" asked Scrooge.

"Shortly, in my new form, Ebenezer, as Jeffery."

"Be serious with me, Jacob. I mean when we each have that luminous form."

"Not only you and I, but friends of other lives will be recognized; and this teaches us the indestructibility of Love, Ebenezer."

"My past record of love isn't too good," said Scrooge.

"It's improved recently," replied Marley.

"Might I hope for more handsome features?" asked Scrooge.

"There, beauty is known as a spiritual quality and little importance is attached to facial features. However, those at the levels of sustained Light have the privilege of costuming themselves at will in new, colorful luminous forms. The same is true for the creation of things. Terrestrial solids must be changed into liquid or other forms through natural or chemical processes, but there, change is by the will of the inhabitants."

The backdoor of the house that led to the garden slammed and Marley abruptly stopped talking. Marley leaned back into the chair, and Scrooge noticed the finger he had used to light the fire had a charred color. He felt that this last conversation with Marley had ended. He was right.

"It will not be very long before the child is born, Ebenezer," said Marley. "This will be the last time you see me. I shall no longer visit with you."

"I understand, Jacob," said Scrooge. "But I shall miss you."

"A spirit will come to you later, with a final message for you," said Marley.

"You're always announcing spirit visitations when you depart from me, Jacob. Why am I so privileged?"

"What makes you think you are the only one?" replied Marley.

"Well," began Scrooge, "I assume . . ."

"Don't," said Marley. "Just accept. Even the longest road ends, Ebenezer. Those unseen roads we have travelled together these many years end in a short time. Soon our roles will be reversed: you will be teaching me, and I shall listen. At least, I hope Kathleen's baby inherits good listening qualities from her and Fred. I'm stuck with whatever physical abilities I get."

"This, then, is the last time we meet," said Scrooge.

"Yes. This is our last meeting, old friend," said Marley. "But every end is a beginning. Marley patted Scrooge on his hand again for the last time. He walked outside onto the brick walk and turned toward the garden. Scrooge watched the specter of Jacob Marley fade among the leafless bushes. He stood motionless for several minutes reliving these last moments with Jacob, recounting what he had heard.

"Uncle Ebenezer! Come quickly! I need you!" The voice was Kathleen's and it came from the garden.

VII

Kathleen had gone out into the garden to find the large flowerpot she needed for the royal fern Fred had given her during their courtship. The fern's compound leaves with narrowly oblong leaflets had spread too far past the edge of the flowerpot for stability, and its near five-foot height made ludicrous the flowerpot, from which it bulged.

Scrooge found Kathleen on her hands and knees. "What is it Kathleen?" he asked. He helped her to stand and noticed a charcoal smudge on the right sleeve of her white blouse.

"I shouldn't have lifted the pot," she said. "I think I strained myself and I think my water broke. It might have been too much for the baby. I may be going into labor, Uncle Ebenezer."

By this time Bertha and Nancy, the cook and the maid, had rushed out to see what was the matter. They helped Scrooge to carry Kathleen to her bed. Scrooge sent Nancy to bring Doctor Chamberlain "immediately!" and ordered Bertha to "boil water, lots of water." Scrooge had no idea why hot water was always needed when babies were born, but at times like this, men, other than the doctor, could do little but "order lots of hot water." Scrooge forgot about Fred.

Nancy ran the entire seven blocks to Dr. Chamberlain's home, where a side entrance led into his back office. She pulled the poor old man, the entire seven blocks, while he attempted to throw his scarf about his neck with one hand and hold his black medical satchel in the other. The faded initials A. B. C. (Anthony Bertrand Chamberlain) that had once been bright golden letters and the myriad cracks in the leather of the satchel that resembled the skin of a venerable black moor, gave evidence of a long practice. That Dr. Chamberlain had to sit down and catch his breath after "that marathon I've been pulled through," also gave evidence that he was well past his prime.

Scrooge urged Dr. Chamberlain to go immediately to Mrs. Langdon's bedroom, and when it appeared that he also might pull the good doctor by his elbow, the cowed doctor reluctantly got up for his own safety.

Regaining his medical authority, Dr. Chamberlain stopped Scrooge from going into Kathleen's bedroom with him. "You sit there!" he ordered Scrooge.

The "there" Doctor Chamberlain pointed to was a meridienne French Empire sofa that Fred had purchased at an auction shortly after their marriage. Kathleen placed it in the hallway directly across from her bedroom door. Scrooge obediently sat down on its red crushed velvet and reclined his head on the arm that was higher than the other was.

A half-hour passed and Scrooge dozed. Suddenly he awoke. "Fred!" he remembered. He told Nancy to fetch Mr. Langdon from his office immediately. Poor Nancy had used up most of her "immediate" energy, but good heart that she was, she scurried the ten blocks to Fred's office, trotting rather than galloping, as the cabbie would say.

Ten minutes later, Doctor Chamberlain closed Kathleen's bedroom door and shook Scrooge, who had again dozed off. "You're Mrs. Langdon's uncle?" he asked. "I'm Mr. Langdon's uncle," Scrooge replied.

"Mrs. Langdon is doing fine," said Doctor Chamberlain. "The baby is due anytime. Where is Mr. Langdon?"

"Nancy has gone to fetch him," replied Scrooge.

"When she returns, I'll need her help." Dr. Chamberlain went back to Kathleen's bedroom.

During the next hour, Fred came home, Nancy went to help Doctor Chamberlain, Bertha kept bringing up more boiling water, and the loud cry of an infant sounded throughout the house.

"You may go in now, for a few minutes. Mrs. Langdon needs rest," said Doctor Chamberlain to Fred.

Fred motioned with his hand for Scrooge to come with him, but Scrooge, conscious of paternal privilege, shook his head no. Fred insisted and took Scrooge by the arm.

Simple exclamations replaced useless sentences, after Fred lovingly kissed Kathleen on the forehead. The baby: cute, beautiful, adorable, beautiful again, cute again. Scrooge smiled, wiped away a tear, and wondered whether in this tiny babe, with its red, soft body rhythmically jerking, lodged the soul of one Scrooge had known as Jacob Marley. His eyes asked Kathleen if he might touch the child. She nodded and smiled.

Slowly Scrooge placed his weathered, wrinkled hand near the child and with two fingers gently lifted its tiny index finger. The small hand stretched open and then fell on the back of Scrooge's hand. It quivered for a moment as if it were patting Scrooge's hand, and then formed a tight fist and pulled back. "Jacob!" whispered Scrooge to himself.

Both Kathleen and Fred smiled. "Jeffery, Uncle Scrooge," said Fred.

"Yes. He's Jeffery," replied Scrooge. He patted the tiny hand with his one finger, smiled at Kathleen and returned to his seat on the sofa, resting thoughtfully on the larger arm.

During the next three months, Scrooge sat by the cradle most of the day, dozing, reading, and during those few moments when Jeffery was awake, without needing to be fed, talking to him before rocking him to sleep again.

"What does he talk to Jeffery about?" Fred asked Kathleen.

"What he reads in the newspaper, the latest gossip from the "Cat and Fiddle" and a lot of stories about when he was in business with Mr. Marley."

"With Mr. Marley?" said Fred. "Well, Jeffery's too young to be bored," said Fred.

"I'm not so sure," laughed Kathleen. "Every time I check on those two and find Uncle Ebenezer talking, Jeffery seems never to take his eyes off of him. Yesterday I even heard Jeffery and Uncle Ebenezer laughing together. Others may have their nanny; we have Uncle Ebenezer."

The long white dress had been Fred's when he was baptized, and now his son would wear it for his baptism.

Jeffery's red hair obviously came from his mother's flowing auburn locks and his dark eyes from his father. He was to be christened Jeffery Vandyke Langdon. Vandyke was his mother's maiden name.

Scrooge remembered the silver chain Marley had given him. He opened the box and noticed for the first time that a tiny silver letter "J" hung from the chain. He didn't recall seeing it the first time he looked at it. Had it originally been intended for "Jacob" or intended now of "Jeffery?" He had learned not to concern himself with slight aberrations in the machinations of Marley, if they were harmless, and particularly if they were fitting. Besides, Kathleen would decide whether Jeffery would wear it. She was delighted. Scrooge hoped his efforts met with Jacob's approval. Or would it be Jeffery's approval?

At Christmas, Scrooge held Jeffery close to the tree and explained what all the different ornaments meant. The tiny blue bird Jeffery grabbed from its perch on a long branch was offered to Scrooge with a giggle. Scrooge described all the figures in the crèche that was displayed below the tree, and to the surprise of Fred and Kathleen, Jeffery appeared interested, particularly when Scrooge picked up the angel behind the figures of Mary and Joseph, and Jeffery reached for it. None of the other pieces Scrooge showed him seemed to interest him.

Christmas Eve or not, Jeffery went to bed after they had all eaten, and Scrooge, holding a special place in his heart for Christmas Eve, excused himself for going to bed so early. After preparing for bed, Scrooge snuffed out his single candle, but did not go to bed. He moved his chair in front of the window and watched a full moon move from pane to pane with each pane, a vision from the past.

Scrooge had fallen asleep in the chair, dreaming about that Christmas long, long ago, when his friends left for the holidays, while he remained. The school bell rang and he opened his eyes. The peal of the church bell rang twelve midnight. The moon had long past the last pane and only nature's small creatures called out.

A soft voice spoke. "Ebenezer?"

"Yes. I am awake. Who is it?" asked Scrooge. Not unexpected, the voice, Scrooge knew, was not human, but with his recent attunement with nature's harmony, he felt not fear, but assurance. "Please, Spirit, make yourself known," he said.

A childlike creature in white, appeared in front of the windows, and the light that glowed around it, slowly filled the room. The sleeves of its garment covered its hands and the cowl, its face.

"Are you the spirit I was told to expect?" asked Scrooge.

"I am," the spirit replied.

"I feared you would be in black and that I had met you two years ago this Christmas Eve," said Scrooge.

"That was my twin, my opposite, my shadow. He is much busier than I am these days. Few are offered the opportunity your partner Jacob Marley brought you that Christmas Eve, and of those that are offered it, only a few accept it," replied the spirit.

"I think I know why you are here." said Scrooge.

"Are you ready, then?" asked the spirit.

"Yes. I should like to see Christmas, however."

The spirit patted Scrooge on his hand and removed the cowl of his garment from his head. The spirit's skin was a pale blue and its hair a mass of golden curls. Compassion flowed from its blue eyes and kindness from its smiling lips. "You shall see Christmas, Ebenezer. Your cycle ends a month before the day set by Fred and Kathleen, to go to Brighton," said the spirit.

Brighton? Why not? A second son is a natural occurrence. Perfect for "big brother" Jeffery. Wonderful for Fred and Kathleen. But it could be a girl! But if his time is a month before they go to Brighton, he'll not see the boy. Or girl. There is a parting in the forks of the road. Things end. He has his own road to travel.

"The fork in the road you conjure in your mind is not as simple as you think, Ebenezer," said the spirit. You have a choice, something rarely obtained." Scrooge sat up. "Something rarely obtained" held his attention. The spirit continued.

"You may remain in Light for an aeon or you may return in ten months to your shadow world, as did your partner Jacob Marley. The choice is yours."

"An aeon? Yes. By all means. That is what I choose, spirit." The spirit said nothing, and a second thought came to Scrooge. "As a matter of curiosity, spirit, where would this return occur and who would be the parents?"

"Here. The parents would be your nephew and niece."

His frame of mind had precluded any such possibility as this, and Scrooge sat dismayed. Human affection still held him from total divine assumption. He would belong to Fred and Kathleen. Jacob would be his brother. David Garrick had played the roles of kindred kings. Why not Scrooge, if not kingly, at least kindred.

"Spirit," said Scrooge sheepishly "I've changed my mind. Ten months is fine."

"You affirm your wish to return in ten months?"

"I do."

"Let it be sealed with this mark." The spirit gently pressed its thumb on the center of Scrooge's forehead. "So mote it be," it said and vanished.

Christmas morning, Scrooge found himself sleeping once again in his chair. He splashed cold water over his face and looked into the mirror. He needed to comb his hair and shave. He moved closer to the mirror. There was a dot on his forehead. A golden dot. He rubbed it with a cloth, but it did not come off. Water and rough scrubbing did not remove it.

He willingly accepted that his experience that evening was not some illusion, some dream, but a momentary opening into the world of Light. This conspicuous golden dot was an unnecessary reminder.

He scratched at it this time, but with no success. What could he do? He would say it was an old Saxon Christmas tradition. Comfortable with this answer, he dressed special for Christmas breakfast with Fred and Kathleen.

Bertha had prepared a full English breakfast that sat on the mahogany buffet, another auction purchase by Fred: scrambled eggs, fried potatoes, beans, sliced tomatoes, sausage patties, fruit, toast, jam, and butter. No questions followed the morning greetings and none came after Scrooge sat down to eat. They were being kind, intending not to embarrass him with questions. The dot was too bright and large, not to be noticed.

They might think this was some bizarre behavior of his in his old age. He would explain it. He pointed to his forehead. "It's an old Saxon Christmas tradition."

"What is an old tradition, Uncle Ebenezer?" asked Fred.

"The dot. The golden dot," replied Scrooge, again pointing to his forehead.

"What dot?" Fred asked.

Scrooge got up and walked to the Federal mirror behind the buffet. The dot was gone. He picked up a roll and placed it on his plate. "How is Jeffery this Christmas morning?" he asked.

The cold winds from the North brought much snow to London that year of 1846-47, which kept Scrooge at home, dozing, reading, rocking the cradle, and talking, endlessly to Jeffery, who now was awake more hours than before. Jeffery walked between tight grips on assorted furniture and even said a few words. His "gra pah" was close enough to "grandpa" for Scrooge, who delighted in teaching him new words. His extended tours of walking, however, tired Scrooge, who tried to keep up with him. Talking proved easier than walking.

Jeffery now sat in a high chair on the side of the table next to his mother, but adjacent to Scrooge, who liked to feed him. A March sun had melted the snow and made travel easier. "Incidentally, Uncle Scrooge, Kathleen, and I are planning a short two day vacation in a few months and have arranged for Mrs. Somerset to take care of Jeffery, while we are gone. We hope you'll supervise things for us then," said Fred.

Scrooge recalled that the spirit said, "A month before they go to Brighton." He kept buttering his toast without thinking. "And where are you and Kathleen going, Fred?" asked Scrooge.

"Why, to Brighton, Uncle Ebenezer," said Fred. "We enjoyed our few days there two years ago."

The next question would tell him how many days he had remaining. "When will you be going?" Scrooge asked. He had put the first piece of toast on his plate and began buttering another piece.

"What are the dates, Kathleen?" asked Fred.

"The tenth and eleventh of May, Dear," replied Kathleen.

Scrooge sat back in his chair. That meant the tenth of April. He had a month to live.

During the next few days, Scrooge spent less time with Jeffery and more time at his desk, arranging papers and letters for his solicitor. He found the other watch-fob he and Jacob had purchased shortly after they had become partners. They had seen the two side-by-side in the window of Carlton's Jewelry Shop just off Piccadilly Circus. To celebrate the occasion, they decided to buy the identical watch-fobs, one engraved with the initial "J" and the other with the initial "E." Jacob's was one of the many things he left to Scrooge.

A week later, Scrooge spoke with Fred in the kiosk in the center of the garden. He explained that he had made final arrangements for Fred to be beneficiary of all his holdings and possessions. As a barrister, Fred was acquainted with Scrooge's solicitor, Horace Dawkins. He should not hesitate to contact Dawkins, should something happen to Scrooge. Although Fred insisted that he looked the picture of health, Scrooge said he had not been feeling well lately.

Scrooge asked Fred to follow him to his rooms, where he showed him the watch-fob that had been Marley's. "I would like for Jeffery to have this. It has a "J" engraved on it." He took his duplicate watch-fob from his pocket. "Someday you may have another son. I would like for him to have this." He placed both watches in the top drawer of his desk and closed it.

"One more request, Fred," said Scrooge, as they walked back to the garden kiosk. "If I should depart this world before your trip to Brighton, don't put it off."

"You're going to be fine, Uncle Ebenezer," said Fred.

"But you promise?" asked Scrooge.

"Yes. Of course," said Fred, more seriously.

The morning of April tenth came. Nothing. Lunch. Nothing. Dinner. Again, nothing. Scrooge sat in his chair and watched the sun go down. Nothing. The church bells rang twelve midnight. Nothing. In spite of the golden dot, it must have been only a dream. He went to bed.

VIII

The next morning, sunlight crossed Scrooge's face, awakening him. It's the eleventh of April. He jumped out of bed and opened the window, taking a deep breath of spring air. He felt good. He looked in the mirror. His reflection was that of a young man. A closer look and it was he thirty years ago. His confusion turned to surprise when he glanced at the side of the chair. Someone was sitting in it!

This was too much. He armed himself with his cane. "Who are …" he began. He stooped, dropped his cane. He was sitting in his chair, slumped over. He had died on the tenth after all.

He could jump higher than ever before. His face was smooth, nearly like Jeffery's. The numbness in his fingers was gone. His shoulders did not bend over. His hair was fuller and darker. All the pleasures without the pains. Why death was living!

Hello, governeur!" She stepped up to Scrooge and placed a white rose in the top buttonhole of his nightgown. "I'm your guide," she said.

"You're the little flower girl!" exclaimed Scrooge.

"I was the little flower girl, but I'm your temporary guide now. You rejected your aeon designation for a return. Is that correct?" she asked. Her cockney had become received English.

"I expect to enter the child of Fred and Kathleen Langdon, that will be conceived in Brighton the tenth of May," said Scrooge.

"Then it is correct that you choose to return?"

"Yes," said Scrooge.

"Well, Ebenezer, since your choice occurs shortly, you will be an observer, but not a resident of either the material world or the spirit world during that time. That is why I am your guide," said the flower girl.

"Does that mean I can be in either world?" asked Scrooge.

"Yes, but unnoticed in either," she replied. "Be wise as to which you observe. Your presence in the material world is required for a successful return."

"May I safely observe in the spiritual world for a short time?" asked Scrooge.

"A short time, Ebenezer. Your inner guide will replace me now, but you may recall me anytime, by touching the rose I gave you." An instant later, she vanished.

Observing the spiritual world proved not the joy expected in residency, but curiosity required it. It was like the child looking at the candy displayed in the front window, while residency was like the child buying candy in the store. Scrooge observed projections of forgotten dreams, remembered acquaintances, cherished possessions, foolish ambitions, and even spiritual fantasies. But candy bought in the store has flavor unequal to the most delectable sweets in the window, and Scrooge responded to his obligation to observe the material world.

At first, Scrooge thought he would observe in Brighton, until Fred and Kathleen came on the tenth and eleventh of May. Several weeks, however, was too long, and he decided to observe them and his old chambers in their home before accompanying them to Brighton. His part wouldn't begin until a "certain creative process took place." This was as much a description as Victorian mores permitted.

Two weeks after his death, Scrooge "returned" to his rooms at Fred and Kathleen's house. While they were no longer his rooms, they had not been touched. Fred and Kathleen mourned for their Uncle Ebenezer in this manner, as well as through the black dresses Kathleen wore and the black armband Fred wore. Scrooge would have preferred a less somber reception.

Scrooge attended their meals with them, although the conversation was subdued. He did not involve himself in what they spoke about. However, one morning their conversation had devastating results.

"I requested a refund on our coach fare to Brighton, my dear," said Fred. "It is too soon after Uncle Ebenezer's death. He must have had a premonition of his death, asking me to promise to go to Brighton, even if something should happen to him."

"He would understand," said Kathleen.

No, he wouldn't! This could not be! Scrooge had chosen return in place of Light for an aeon! Return to the child they would conceive in Brighton on the tenth of this month. If this didn't occur, he might end up in some intermediary state between limbo and purgatory, waiting an aeon for another choice. How did this happen? Initially he had appreciated the apparent order within the spirit world as compared to the periodic chaos of the material world. But this! Unacceptable.

In the ensuing two weeks, Scrooge did everything he could imagine to change their minds, to encourage them to go to Brighton as planned on the tenth and eleventh of this month, May. As soul, Scrooge would be near the new life that would conceive in Brighton on the tenth. Order should prevail. The time and place was established. The child would be born. Certainly a boy. He would see to that in the important nine months. He would also manage to have Fred and Kathleen name the boy Edmund.

He whispered in each of their ears. He suggested thoughts during their quiet time. He induced his visions of Brighton and transferred his imaginations to each of them. He practiced the mantra, "Uncle Scrooge won't mind. Uncle Scrooge won't mind," with no success. They would show their respect for Uncle Scrooge, by staying home. It was the twelfth of May. Scrooge was despondent. He touched the white rose.

"What has happened?" Scrooge asked her as soon as she materialized.

"Nothing unexpected," she replied. "You assumed the new life you were to be near on the tenth of May, had to be conceived in Brighton. The tenth was correct. Your assumption that it was to occur in Brighton is not correct. It was London."

"London? But they didn't leave London," said Scrooge.

The flower girl smiled and withdrew the white rose. "Now you must listen only to your inner guide, Ebenezer. Your work should have begun two days ago."

During the next nine months, Scrooge never left the house or Kathleen, while always respecting her privacy. Scrooge's required presence most of the time by or near Kathleen during her pregnancy seemed uncomplicated, even simple. Scrooge, however, soon discovered that not to be the case.

First, there is the mother. Kathleen's sudden craving for pickles at three in the morning not only involved Fred, who had to find them in the kitchen, but also Scrooge, who needed to inform Kathleen that the sugar in sweet pickles would have an adverse effect on the tiny life she was nurturing. He whispered as loud as he could into her ear and the message was finally heard. Fred had to go back to the kitchen and find dill pickles.

The nurturing life force, though powerful, did not itself evaluate, with the consequence that certain cell, tissue, nerve, and organ development needed to cease, increase, slow down, speed up, or stop. These decisions depended on Scrooge, on the input he obtained from his inner guide and his skill in manipulating the nurturing life force.

The most complicated input to confront Scrooge occurred about the sixth month, when the living mass of cells had developed into a recognizably tiny human creature with a primitive "will" of its own. It moved its arms, its legs, sucked its thumb, and kicked its unsuspecting mother in the stomach. This primitive will had to be subdued and eventually assumed by the hovering soul, in this case, Scrooge.

The final challenge occurred during the last few hours before birth, when the fully developed child intuitively sensed that it was soon to be expelled from the comfort and security of its special place. When this reluctance was overcome, birth soon followed, and then immediately, with the first cry, Scrooge as soul, became absorbed with the first breath and was sucked into body and lungs, with all memory now confined to the subconscious of a new human being.

The partner that had been Marley's and the recipient of his counsel had ceased ten months ago; and now, with his death in the spirit world, he was born anew as Edmund, on February 21, 1848.

Fred and Kathleen wanted their new baby to be welcomed by Jeffery and in no way, be a threat to their love for him. Although

Jeffery was less than two years old, they explained to him that he would soon have a little brother. The baby was born at home with no difficulty and on the second day after its birth, Jeffery was brought in to see his "baby brother."

Jeffery looked with the eyes of a child at Christmas, but the toy moved, gyrated, cried. He reached through the crib and gently touched this new toy. It was warm, soft; Fred and Kathleen watched for minutes, as Jeffery became absorbed in his "baby brother."

Jeffery looked up to his parents and spoke several phrases.

"What is he saying?" Kathleen asked Fred.

"It sounds like 'e-bee.' He keeps saying 'e-bee, e-bee nees-er.' He's trying to say, 'The baby needs her.' He must think the baby needs you. Isn't that remarkable for a two year old?"

Jeffery placed his hand again into the crib and patted the hand of his baby brother. "E-bee nee-zer," he said.

EPILOGUE

Samuel Johnson was asked what he thought of David Garrick's portrayal of Macbeth; Boswell reported what he said, although it is probably apocryphal and is not in his autobiography, of Johnson. According to Boswell, Johnson replied that Garrick didn't play the part, but Hamlet did. He meant Garrick's portrayal of Macbeth had too much of his previous portrayal of Hamlet.

The same was true of Jeffery and Edmund Langdon. The silver cord had not been completely severed and both retain memories as Jacob or Ebenezer. By the time each become three, such memories, however, sank into their subconscious and they became Jeffery and Edmund.

Like his father, Jeffery entered the legal profession and became a barrister. Clever, ambitious, he married the daughter of the then Secretary of War Campbell-Bannerman, who later served Edward VII as Prime Minister. The year after their marriage, they had a son, whom they named Charles.

At forty-two, Jeffery became part of Gladstone's cabinet in 1892, and two years later went to India with his wife to serve Lord Elgin, who became Viceroy of India in 1894. Charles remained at home with his Uncle Edmund. Jeffery returned to England in 1896, the year his wife died. A year later he died.

Edmund entered the medical profession and studied under Doctor Timothy Cratchet. At twenty-two, Edmund had fallen in love with Emma Boyeln. While they were crossing a busy intersection at

Fleet Street, a runaway horse and carriage ran over Emma, killing her instantly, and severely injured Edmund. He never married.

Edmund had been appointed guardian of Jeffery's son Charles, in Jeffery's will. Charles married in 1905 when he was twenty-two, the same age as Edmund, when his fiancée was killed. Charles had been concerned that he was too young to marry. "Marry her," advised Edmund.

Charles and his wife planned to take their two children Stephen, age 8, and Emily, age six, on a vacation to Brighton and asked Edmund to go with them. He accepted, not because he would be with Charles and his wife, but because he would be with Stephen and Emily. They were more his grandchildren than they were Jeffery's.

Early the first morning in Brighton, Edmund rose with the sun and walked to the beach. He found a large rock and sat on it, watching the gulls, the ebbing shoreline, and the distant ships. Edmund felt at peace, a peace not of the moment, but of the timeless surge of the sea. A gull flew up to him and sat on the rock. He spoke to the gull, which then flapped its wet wings and flew away.

That afternoon he watched Stephen on a white horse, a fine silver chain around his neck from which a tiny, worn, silver "J" hung, and Emily in a red sled, ride the merry-go-round. After two rides, Stephen wanted to know why the older boy next to him kept reaching for something every time he came to the red column. Edmund explained that attached to the red column was a golden ring. If the boy, or any rider, on the merry-go-round could grab the ring, he would win a prize. Stephen spent all the change Edmund had, riding the merry-go-round. Stephen reached for the ring with every turn, but his reach was always too short.

Edmund held Emily, who had become tired, and enjoyed watching Stephen during his next twelve rides. He explained to Stephen, disappointed at not getting the ring, that when he was grown up he would be able to grab the golden ring. But then Edmund realized that Stephen would no longer want to.

We go round and round, each time missing the golden ring; and then when we are older, when we can reach it, we don't care. But someday, some year, someone, a shadow of Scrooge and an image of Edmund, will intentionally reach farther and grasp the golden ring.

###

ABOUT THE AUTHOR

Karl F. Hollenbach was born in 1925 in Louisville, Kentucky. He received his B.A. and M. Ed. from the University of Louisville. His esoteric and metaphysical articles have been published in Japan and England as well as the United States. He and his artist wife live on Dunsinane Hill Farm near Fort Knox, Kentucky.

Additional information about the author may be found at http://BooksAuthorsAndArtists.com and on the Books, Authors and Artists Facebook page at https://www.facebook.com/BooksAuthorsAndArtists

Also by Karl F. Hollenbach

A JOURNEY TO THE FOUR KINGDOMS
    Amazon Kindle ebook: http://amzn.to/YCQpwJ
    Amazon paperback: http://amzn.to/15l16lg
    CreateSpace paperback: https://www.createspace.com/4136583

ANECDOTES AND SPECIAL NOTES
    Amazon Kindle ebook: http://amzn.to/16pgHtU
    Amazon paperback: http://amzn.to/10Dmb1v
    CreateSpace paperback: https://www.createspace.com/4278307

PATTON: MANY LIVES, MANY BATTLES
    Amazon Kindle ebook: http://amzn.to/XIjvsm
    Amazon paperback: http://amzn.to/WFENtl
    CreateSpace paperback: https://www.createspace.com/4097702

MANSIONS OF THE MOON (formerly ERICIUS)
    Amazon Kindle ebook: http://amzn.to/1gYq8p6
    Amazon paperback: http://amzn.to/1f8r2yy
    CreateSpace paperback: https://www.createspace.com/4428046

FRANCIS ROSICROSS
>Amazon Kindle ebook: http://amzn.to/1klGlGu
>Amazon paperback: http://amzn.to/1d3pzIi
>CreateSpace paperback: https://www.createspace.com/4521941

HANDBOOK – APPLYING METAPHYSICAL PRINCIPLES IN TEACHING
>Amazon Kindle ebook: http://amzn.to/Ysuo3o
>Amazon paperback: http://amzn.to/Y1O6Df
>CreateSpace paperback: https://www.createspace.com/4035946

THE GREAT HAWK
>Amazon Kindle ebook: http://amzn.to/Z9TCo5
>Amazon paperback: http://amzn.to/1513XGb
>CreateSpace paperback: https://www.createspace.com/4044068

THE RIGHTEOUS ROGUE
>Amazon Kindle ebook: http://amzn.to/12QAMWD
>Amazon paperback: http://amzn.to/13CHeiD
>CreateSpace paperback: https://www.createspace.com/4247817

THRICE TOLD TALES
>Amazon Kindle ebook: http://amzn.to/17YzgH5
>Amazon paperback: http://amzn.to/14wpXZV
>CreateSpace paperback: https://www.createspace.com/4280447

THRICE TOLD TALES: LARGE PRINT EDITION
>Amazon Kindle ebook: http://amzn.to/1jBlTzW
>Amazon paperback: http://amzn.to/1eblTEg
>CreateSpace paperback: https://www.createspace.com/4614310

How to Contact Karl F.:

Goodreads:
http://www.goodreads.com/search?utf8=%E2%9C%93&q=Karl+F.+Hollenbach&search_type=books

Publisher's Facebook:
https://www.facebook.com/BooksAuthorsAndArtists

Amazon's Author's Page:
http://www.amazon.com/Karl-F.-
Hollenbach/e/B00B36VS38/ref=sr_tc_2_0?qid=1363387919&sr=1-2-ent

Where to purchase books by Karl F. Hollenbach:
Please see the Amazon and CreateSpace links under each title above.

YOUR REVIEW IS IMPORTANT!

We appreciate your support for Karl F.

In advance, we are very grateful for your review of any of his works.
Please post a review, with your analysis, thoughts, and ideas at:

Amazon:
http://amzn.to/XWgQPs

Goodreads:
http://www.goodreads.com/book/show/16153184-scrooge-and-marley

The author, Karl F. Hollenbach, interviews Ebenezer Scrooge.

AUTHOR: I am led to understand that you had a dream about ghosts and spirits, Mr. Scrooge.

SCROOGE: A visitation, sir, not a dream. I was fully awake each time.

AUTHOR: How can you be sure, Mr. Scrooge?

SCROOGE: Are you awake now, sir, or are you sleeping?

AUTHOR: I understand your point. Can you describe your experience?

SCROOGE: As easily as I may describe the other events I experienced that same day.

AUTHOR: Your experience, your visitations, occurred at night, did they not?

SCROOGE: They did. The first visitation was my business partner, Jacob Marley.

AUTHOR: Was it not his ghost, Mr. Scrooge?

SCROOGE: Ghost is a more frightening term than spirit. It is an Anglo-Saxon word, while spirit is a Latin word, which is a more agreeable word for non-physical beings. What matters is that the personality - soul, if you will -- of Jacob Marley visited me and spoke with me.

AUTHOR: The first time was a Christmas Eve. Is that right, sir?

SCROOGE: Yes. Then he visited me the following Christmas Eve and a number of days after that.

AUTHOR: If you permit me, Mr. Scrooge, since it is your experience, how do you explain it?

SCROOGE: I do not. Marley told me he came from the astral plane that exists beyond the material plane. It is the sphere of non-material existence, but I was not then, nor am I now, interested in an explanation of his presence, but I was and am interested in what he told me.

AUTHOR: And what was that, Mr. Scrooge?

SCROOGE: To be in a state of bliss when I departed this world, I must heed the messages, which were to be given to me by three spirits.

AUTHOR: Not ghosts this time.

SCROOGE: No, not ghosts, but representatives of ideas.

AUTHOR: Metaphors?

SCROOGE: Yes! Very good young man. Metaphors for the joyful spirit children find in Christmas: the hundreds of past Christmases, the Christmas that was to be celebrated the following morning, and all the Christmases in the future. They brought happiness and joy to my soul.

AUTHOR: How is that?

SCROOGE: The visions I saw from the past, present, and future showed me how empty my life was and how full of joy it could be, and, since then, is!

AUTHOR: Mr. Marley visited you the following Christmas. Is that correct

SCROOGE: It certainly is,' and a number of times following that second visit.

AUTHOR: Why do you think this opportunity was given to you?

SCROOGE: What makes you think it isn't given to all lost souls?

AUTHOR: Well, I . . . I'm asking questions today, Mr. Scrooge, not answering them.

SCROOGE: Marley told me many things about the world beyond. He gave me answers to questions I should have asked long before I achieved advanced years. Why we are here. What things are for us to do. What we should first seek.

AUTHOR: I ask myself those questions sometimes, Mr. Scrooge.

SCROOGE: Have you received answers, young man?

AUTHOR: Well, I'm not sure there are answers.

SCROOGE: Come with me to the Inn, young man, for a cup of hot grog, and I will tell you what the third Spirit told me during his second visit.

AUTHOR: I thought the third spirit did not speak?

SCROOGE: But he did! Not to my mind and my ears, but to my heart and soul. Come, let us be off.

###

The author, Karl F. Hollenbach, interviews Bob Cratchet

AUTHOR: Mr. Cratchet. . .

CRATCHET: Please, call me Bob.

AUTHOR: Bob ... you probably knew Mr. Scrooge better than anyone during his adult life.

CRATCHET: You are correct, sir, I have been in his employ for nearly twenty years, the only clerk at Scrooge and Marley.

AUTHOR: The business is now Scrooge, Marley, and Cratchet. Is that not right Mr. . . . . Bob?

CRATCHET: Yes, shortly after Mr. Scrooge's "change" he made me a partner.

AUTHOR: You use the word, change. Can you tell me about that?

CRATCHET: Well,' sir, it was a most strange and wondrous thing that happened to Mr. Scrooge. He was a fair man, a man of his word, but how shall I say it ... he was not a friendly man. Everything was business. He was not married, you know. Some called him a skinflint, some a miser, but I thought of him as a lonely old gentleman who had no one to love or no one to love him.

AUTHOR: He has a nephew, I believe?

CRATCHET: Oh, Master Fred is a fine nephew. Visited his uncle every Christmas Eve to invite him to his house for Christmas dinner, and always wished him a Merry Christmas even when Mr. Scrooge would tell him it was a humbug. That was a favorite expression Mr. Scrooge called about everything that brings happiness to people.

AUTHOR: Didn't Mr. Scrooge live with his nephew and his wife Kathleen after his—what you called it—change?

CRATCHET: He did, sir. And was loved by Mrs. Kathleen.

AUTHOR: You started telling me about Mr. Scrooge's change

CRATCHET: It was quite sudden, young man. One day Mr. Scrooge was - all business and the next day -- completely the opposite. For years, Mr. Scrooge appeared to be unhappy about giving me Christmas day off, the next time he wanted me to go home early on Christmas Eve. Miserly when I asked for a small raise, he later made me his partner.

AUTHOR: Can you tell me more about this abrupt change?

CRATCHET: Well sir, when Mr. Scrooge departed our house after joining my family for Charismas dinner, he said something about "parting," I thought. With all the noise and revelry from my children, I couldn't hear all he said and merely nodded my head yes, and smiled. I did not realize that he wanted to surprise me just before leaving by informing me that I was to be his partner in Scrooge and Marley.

The next morning I arrived later than usual, and hurried to my desk. "Well?" asked Mr. Scrooge, with a questioning smile on his face "The holidays, Mr. Scrooge. It won't happen again," was my rather tremulous excuse.

"Didn't you see it, man?" exclaimed Mr. Scrooge. I was becoming puzzled. "See what, Mr. Scrooge?" I asked. I became afraid Mr. Scrooge was seeing ghosts again.

"Go outside, Cratchet," instructed Mr. Scrooge. My bewildered look required him to add, "Look up, always look up, but particularly at the sign!"

A partner! Now I understood what Mr. Scrooge was smiling about. On the other hand, did I? I rushed back into the office and could only stammer, "I . . . I . . ." Until Mr. Scrooge said, "Bob, take the rest of the day off and celebrate with your family."

AUTHOR: How do you explain the change?

CRATCHET: For Mr. Scrooge, no lost soul is every forgotten. For me, I never allowed myself to become bitter. I always try to appreciate what I have, a loving wife, a beautiful family and even Mr. Scrooge is, was, consistently and predictably of a certain demeanor. Mr. Scrooge's sudden transformation tells me that a soul is never lost, simply misdirected for a time.

###

The author interviews Misters Prynne and Chelmsford, the solicitors for Christmas gift funds, Miss Nettie Straw, the charwoman, Miss Charlotte Cope, the housekeeper, and Alfred, the waiter at the "Cat and Fiddle" Inn.

AUTHOR: Thank you for coming to this short interview. I would like to begin by speaking with the two of you, Mr. Prynne and Mr. Chelmsford. You both solicited Christmas gift funds from Mr. Ebenezer Scrooge.

MR.CHELMSFORD: Thank you for inviting us. That is true, but we were originally unsuccessful. When I asked Mr. Scrooge how much we could put him down for, he replied, "Nothing!" "Ah!" I said, "You wish to be anonymous." Mr. Scrooge rather pointedly stated, "I wish to be left alone!"

MR. PRYNNE: His stern features and brisk manner bespoke of an unhappy man: As you can well surmise, we left.

MR. CHELMSFORD: After wishing the dour Mr. Scrooge a Merry Christmas!, remember, Mr. Prynne?

MR. PRYNNE: We encountered Mr. Scrooge the next day on the streets, an event we would have avoided if possible. However, this Mr. Scrooge was altogether different - a man who smiled and grasped both our hands, exuding joy, much less holiday happiness. He handed us a goodly amount of money. We were so shocked by the complete change of his ways, that we could stammer only a simple, "Thank you!"

MR. CHELMSFORD: We certainly would not have solicited him the following Christmas if we had not met him for that short time on the streets, when he displayed such a change of manner.

MR. PRYNNE: When we entered his office the next Christmas, we told the clerk we wished to speak with Mr. Scrooge. Before the clerk could answer, Mr. Scrooge bounced - am I right, Chelmsford, he bounced-out of his office and enthusiastically grabbed both our hands.

"I've been waiting for you!" beamed Mr. Scrooge. He thrust a plump envelope into Chelmsford's hand, shaking mine and then Chelmsford's.

"It includes a number of back payments, gentlemen," he said sheepishly but smiling.

AUTHOR: How do you account for such a change?

MR.PRYNNE: A miracle!

MR.CHELMSFORD: Proof that change is possible, I would say.

AUTHOR: Thank you, gentlemen.

AUTHOR: Miss Nettie Straw? You were Mr. Scrooge's charwoman, his part-time house cleaner. Is that correct?

MISS STRAW: Yes. For several years, I replaced Mrs. Dilbert, God rest her soul.

AUTHOR: And you were his housekeeper, Miss Cope?

MISS COPE: Charlotte Cope. Yes. I was his housekeeper for fifteen years, until the kind and generous gentleman passed away.

AUTHOR: He was always kind and good?

MISSES STRAW AND COPE: Oh, no sir!

MISS STRAW: He was a most unkind, selfish man, although not terribly mean spirited, until, all of a sudden, he changed! Isn't that true, Charlotte?

MISS COPE: As sure as Jack followed Jill.

AUTHOR: Tell me about Mr. Scrooge's transformation.

MISS STRAW: Mr. Scrooge always counted every garment I washed and ironed before paying me, and then, one day he thanked me for such fine washing and ironing of his clothing, asked how I was feeling, and gave we an extra bob for my good work!

MISS COPE: Very strange happenings, young man. I always brought crumpets, strawberry jam with clotted cream, and his breakfast tea each morning, and left gruel, usually scones, and made a fire in his room for his Earl Grey in the evening.

The same thing happened to me the very next morning that happened to Nettie. Mr. Scrooge was out of bed, shaved, dressed in his finery, and prancing around the room, like a child on Christmas morn capering around the sparkling Christmas tree.

"Here, let me take the tray, Miss. Cope," says Mr. Scrooge. I seldom saw him, except if I had to shake him awake. What a delicious looking breakfast!" he says. "You do wonders with the simplest of food. Sorry are the men who have allowed you to remain Miss Cope. I was flummoxed, more than a little concerned, and spoke with Nettie as soon as I could.

AUTHOR: What do you think happened to Mr. Scrooge?

MISS STRAW: He must have found and then drunk from the cup of human kindness. Finally!

MISS COPE: At least he found the cup, Nettie.

AUTHOR: Thank you very much ladies.

AUTHOR: You, sir, served Mr. Scrooge at "The Cat and the Fiddle?

ALFRED: Yes, sir. I'm Alfred. I served Mr. Scrooge his evening meal for many years.

AUTHOR: Did you see a difference in Mr. Scrooge at the same time Misses Straw and Cope did, Alfred?

ALFRED: Most definitely. For years Mr. Scrooge would give me his order - usually the same beef and potatoes - and say nothing else to me the rest of his meal. He would leave an extra penny when he paid by for his dinner by leaving the money on the table. On that evening, he called me Alfred, he enquired as to my health, how my wife and children were, - they had grown by then - and asked me what I would recommend for dinner!

Such a change continued through the following year. The next Christmas I began hearing him talk to - well, as if someone was sitting across the booth from him. I will admit to becoming rather fond of the gentleman, who had changed into a kindly, gracious old man. I thought he was - well as they say, just getting along in his years.

AUTHOR: What did you think about such happenings, Alfred?

ALFRED: The Good Lord was testing me. For years, I never allowed myself to become upset with Mr. Scrooge's selfish ways, churlish manner, and pecunious tipping. After many years, I was rewarded.

AUTHOR: What about Mr. Scrooge?

ALFRED: He played his part very well.

AUTHOR: Ladies, gentlemen, thank you very much for sharing your observations of Mr. Scrooge and what you thought of his abrupt transformation. May your day be pleasant and the roles you played in *Scrooge And Marley* be noted and long-remembered.

###